GAME CHANGING MOVES:

Life Lessons from the Locker Room and Beyond

By Chad Parks

Game Changing Moves
ISBN 978-1-938254-65-9

Cross Training Publishing
www.crosstrainingpublishing.com
(308) 293-3891

Copyright © 2017 by Chad Parks

GAME
CHANGING
MOVES

PRAISE FOR

GAME CHANGING MOVES
Life Lessons from the Locker Room and Beyond

"As you dive in and experience this game changing book, you can't help but be captivated by Coach Chad Parks' passion for a greater purpose! It's an uplifting passion that is contagious; it will reignite your flame and reaffirm your faith for the journey. Chad is a true messenger of the word, and that light radiates in each message in a transformational way. As the words flood your heart, you become more aware of your impact, the power of positive reflection, and will be inspired by his ability to create lessons and perspective through the parallels of wrestling and life."

> Cody Garcia
> Head Wrestling Coach at Baker University,
> Two-Time NCAA Champion (2006, 2008)

"As long as I have known Chad, he has been a great man and that comes through clearly in this book. If you are looking for a guide to help you succeed in every area of your life, then you need to look no further. *Game Changing Moves* is a winner."

> Kerry McCoy
> Head Wrestling Coach at the University of Maryland,
> Two-time Olympian (2000, 2004),
> Two-Time NCAA Champion (1994, 1997)

"Engaging. Challenging. Inspiring. Every once in awhile an author comes along with truth and wisdom that transcends sports and life; Chad Parks clearly did just that with *Game Changing Moves*. This book will not only transform your mind, it will strengthen your soul!"

> Dr. Jarrod Spencer
> Founder of MIND OF THE ATHLETE, LLC and the Author of
> *MIND OF THE ATHLETE*

'I am thankful for Chad Parks. He has been a great encouragement in my own writing, and I feel blessed to be a resource for him in return. I think *Game Changing Moves* is a fantastic book! For me, this book embodies three inspiring aspects: faith, wrestling, and life. The chapters are brief and to the point, which allows the reader to take a step back and reflect on the individual messages that are delivered. I found myself taking pauses throughout the course of my reading in order to really think about and consider some of the great wisdom Chad delivers in this material. Reading this book was a "game changing move" in and of itself for me; I encourage others to do the same."

Michael Fessler
Writer, Speaker, and the Author of *Faith and Wrestling*,
They're Just Not Interested and *The Wrestler* .

"Coach Chad Parks reminds us in this book why the superficial elements of sport are not enough. He challenges his readers to invest in the heart and soul of the athlete and gives us evidence of how that can be transformative in a person's life. This is not just a book; it's a real life picture of what we should all be striving for as coaches. Thanks Coach!"

Heath Eslinger
Head Wrestling Coach at the University of Tennessee at Chattanooga. 2x Southern Conference Coach of the Year. Recipient of the FCA Gerry Stephens Influence Award and Jim Sattler Leadership Award.

"*Game Changing Moves* is absolutely pure and transformative. Chad Parks captures the keys to be successful, not just as a wrestler or coach but also a human being. Having had success in both collegiate and international wrestling, I am often asked "How do you become a champion?" My new answer is to start by reading this book!"

Kendric Maple
Undefeated NCAA Wrestling National Champion (2013)
US Open Freestyle Champion (2017)
Assistant Wrestling Coach Purdue University

"This riveting book is replete with tools for success. It arms those who want to succeed with motivation and drive by practical application from real life examples and stories. I highly recommend this book to every person that's ever had a dream to be more than the mundane average."

Venshard Dobbins
Elder and Minister, The Potter's House Church Dallas

"This brilliant book by Coach Chad Parks is the winning game plan to life. A must read for anyone looking for motivation, application and guidance for that game changing move to enhance their sports, professional, business, spiritual and personal journey. This book gives powerful, applicable life lessons through sports, relationships, family with the ideas of discipline, trust, work, servitude, love and faith. A must read on how to be a winner and champion in the game of life."

Mark Humble
Offensive Coordinator and Quarterbacks Coach, Southlake Carroll High School. 8 Time Texas High School Football State Champions

"So many times we hear that lessons learned in sports apply to life in general. Now, you get to actually read and apply those lessons, as told through one of the most successful coaches in our region. Chad Parks does an amazing job of sharing the lessons he's learned in his time competing and coaching in a way that applies to your life. If you want to be more successful, read this book."

Cody Foster
Founder of Advisors Excel

"Are you ready for change, looking for a better you, or desire to strengthen your spiritual life? Then I highly recommend *Game Changing Moves* to help you transform into a better version of yourself. This book is not restricted to athletes or coaches as Chad Parks has touched on all aspects of life for the person ready to produce their own game changing moves!"

Tyler Gonzales
Coordinator of Training Sites and Community Partnership for the
United States Olympic Committee

"Chad Parks nails it with *Game Changing Moves!* This book covers all aspects of life through wrestling and beyond, along with tying in Biblical scripture beautifully throughout. *Game Changing Moves* will challenge you to review your past, live in the present and make positive changes that will impact your future. This book is loaded with great stories and fantastic insight from the world of sports, leadership, and more through the eyes of Chad Parks!

Chas Thompson
Head Wrestling Coach at Fort Hays State University, MIAA Wrestling
Coach of the Year, College All-American Wrestler

Chad Parks is the real deal. These are not just words on a page but authentic life lessons from a friend who practices what he preaches and lives out his faith daily. These life lessons and biblical truths are relevant and applicable to every human being. This book has made my reread stack for its worth and reminder to never lose hope and be a man of faith and action!

RD Cogswell
President of the AIM 5 Foundation

"Coach Parks brings alive his real life experiences as a son, athlete, and coach. I highly recommend this book to all coaches, athletes, and leaders who value their time and want to truly make a difference. Be a difference maker!"

Joe Hadachek
AdvoCare International Hall of Fame, Head Football Coach
Union Community, IA

"There is no better sport than wrestling to teach a person about overcoming the trials and tribulations of life. Life isn't fair and is rarely easy, and that philosophy is identical to wrestling. Just because you have trained harder than your opponent doesn't mean the match will be given to you. This book illustrates that multiple times, not just with wrestling but with several aspects of life. Chad Parks gets his hand raised in victory with this book."

Joe Renfro
Head Wrestling Coach at Northeastern Oklahoma A&M College,
Five NJCAA Wrestling National Championships, Six-time NJCAA
Coach of the Year

"Coach Parks does an incredible job of sharing his testimony and love for his athletes in our great sport of wrestling. As a fellow Christian coach, it is encouraging for me to read of the similar struggles and successes Coach Parks has encountered. *Game Changing Moves* is an inspirational book that will keep you hungry to read the next chapter. Fellow Christians and coaches, take advantage of the "Game Changing Moves" at the end of each chapter as I promise they will help you grow in your faith and leadership skills. My team will use this book to supplement our weekly Bible study in order help develop young men into strong Christians. One of our team goals is to honor Christ in all that we do, and this text provides a great reference point to hit that benchmark."

Andrew Nicola
Head Wrestling Coach at Concordia University, USA Wrestling
Freestyle and Greco Roman Veterans National Champion (2016)

DEDICATION

This book is dedicated to Coach Martin Parks and Coach Jody Thompson. You are two of the greatest coaches I know, and I'm grateful for the influence you have in my life. Your guidance has equipped me with game changing moves as an athlete, coach, parent, and leader. Thank you for showing me what it looks like to invest in others with passion and love.

CONTENTS

FOREWORD

THE GAME CHANGER
Tanner Gardner
Senior Associate Athletic Director/CRO, Rice University
Three-time NCAA Wrestling All-American, Stanford University
(2006, 2007, 2008)
Three-time NCAA Academic All-American (2006, 2007, 2008)
Pac-12 Wrestling All-Century Team Selection (Selected 2016)

Life is fast. Life is furious. Life is overwhelming. Do these statements resonate with you? I know they resonate with me.

We all have a series of life experiences that impact who we are today. Whether it be a great accomplishment, a great failure, a great joy or a great tragedy, our lives are shaped by our experiences. However, I believe we often miss the most powerful lessons from these experiences because life gets in the way. We are so busy that we neglect to learn from key moments in our life. Only when we slow down and reflect on our experiences do we learn and grow. I have found this process of self-reflection to be highly impactful in my own life.

I have had the fortune of knowing Coach Parks for almost 15 years. One thing I have always appreciated about Coach Parks is his thoughtfulness and desire to know more as well as become more. This is wonderfully expressed in the text of *Game Changing Moves*. The book provides practical lessons based on real-life experiences. Not only do the lessons provide direction for how to succeed on the field but more broadly provide wisdom that can help you become better in every area of your life. Perhaps most importantly, they are rooted in sound Biblical principles, making the lessons timeless. Reading through *Game Changing Moves*, you will learn from the experiences of the many incredible individuals Coach Parks has interacted with in his life. The lessons gleaned from these experiences are highly applicable to leadership, athletics, coaching, business, and life. As you read through this book, I also encourage you to think about how the ultimate book of game changing moves, the Bible, informs your life. It has had a transformative impact on me, and I know it will do the same for you should you let it.

Coach Parks has written a powerful and impactful book that will help you on the journey to becoming the person God has created you to be. So read, reflect and get ready to experience your own *Game Changing Moves.*

INTRODUCTION

"So Jacob was left alone, and a man wrestled with him till daybreak. When the man saw that he could not overpower him, he touched the socket of Jacob's hip so that his hip was wrenched as he wrestled with the man." Genesis 32:24-25

Twenty, nineteen, eighteen... The seconds ticked off the clock as Austin Willis, my best wrestler, lay facedown on the mat while I sat helplessly in the corner wondering where we had gone wrong. Suddenly the downed wrestler lifted his arm and turned into his opponent, offering the top wrestler an opportunity to seal the victory with a fall. Like a lion moving in for the kill, the mounted wrestler seized his moment, but to his dismay the trap had been sprung. Austin wrapped his arm around the head of his captor, twisted his hips and elevated a leg in one smooth and well rehearsed motion. The top wrestler was flung to his back, and there was no route of escape as his shoulders were pinned to the mat. Slap! Just like that, the referee's palm hit the wrestling surface. The impossible had become possible. Down by 12 points, with seven seconds left on the clock, Austin hit a game changing move and won his first medal in the state wrestling tournament.

Fourteen years prior to this event, I was walking down the hallway of a Missouri Valley College dormitory when a student with a brilliant smiling face approached me with outstretched hand. He introduced himself as Venshard Dobbins (aka Vince), welcomed me to school, and then went on his way. I ended up passing Vince in the hallway several times over the course of the next few months. Each time he greeted me with a smile and a handshake, and addressed me as Brother Chad. Vince also invited me to church several times, but I always found a reason to decline his offer. Then one day, no different than any other day, I ran into Vince and agreed to go to church with him after being asked for the umpteenth time.

I attended church with Vince (a dual sport athlete at Missouri Valley College) not knowing what to expect, but hoping he'd stop asking me to go after that weekend. What I didn't realize was that the trap had sprung, and God himself was about to hit me with a game changing move, just as He had done to Jacob in Genesis 32. During that service I was mentally and emotionally stirred in a way like never before. It's like God wrapped his arm around my head, kicked me upside down, and then gently placed me back on my feet as a changed man. God hit me with a game changing move that allowed Him to win our life long wrestling match and my heart.

I am a coach and a coach's son. When I was two weeks of age, my mother took me to watch my first wrestling match. I was virtually raised in the locker rooms as my dad coached both football and wrestling throughout my youth. In these locker rooms I was trained as an athlete, and the foundation was set for my coaching career. It was also in these locker rooms that I began to understand the power of a game changing move.

Although the game changing move is highly applicable to sports, it is far from locked into that arena. A game changing move applies to every area of our lives, including sports, business and relationships. The game changing move is an action that quickly changes a situation in our favor and has a powerful impact on our personal journey. There are times you will execute a game changing move and times it will be carried out upon you. Sometimes the impact is felt and realized immediately, and at other times the awareness comes later down the road. Either way, the game changing move is powerful and effective.

Throughout this book, I will share with you life lessons I learned through athletics, hard work and building relationships. My hope is you will understand the power of a game changing move. The intention is to give you real, meaningful and applicable tools that help you develop your own game changing moves. Please take the time to read, highlight, write notes and internalize the principles being shared. You will also be provided with guiding questions at the conclusion of each chapter to help you develop your own game changing moves that can be applied to various areas of your life.

Let the journey begin...

RELATIONAL LEADERSHIP

"I love you Coach."

Those are four of the most important and powerful words I heard in my coaching career. Thankfully, I heard them a number of times and from various athletes. Sometimes those exact words are spoken; other times the 'I love you' is shown in actions. Either way, it's powerful.

Why are these words so powerful to me as a coach? It's simple; I love my athletes too. It's about relationship development and relational leadership. I often heard my dad, who is a tremendous coach, say "People don't care what you know until they know that you care." I believe this statement to be true, and I've seen it in action as a teacher, coach and human being. I'm certain we've all seen those words in action throughout our lives.

Relational leadership is about developing relationships with those you lead and letting them know with certainty that you care about them as a person. Not that you care about them because of what you can get out of them or what they can do for you. That is transactional leadership, seeing those you lead as a transaction to get what you want.

Wrestler Nick Meck and Coach Chad Parks talking before the State Finals.(2012)

Thankfully I had a number of coaches who modeled relational leadership for me as an athlete. My own father was (and still is) a master of relational leadership. I can't tell you how many of his former athletes would visit our house when I was a kid because they wanted to visit with Coach Parks. They would return from college on Christmas break and make certain to stop by the house or the wrestling room to talk.

They didn't need to do this, but they loved the man who had made such an impact in their lives.

Another of my coaches to demonstrate relational leadership excellence was my Labette Community College wrestling coach, Jody Thompson, AKA Coach T. Coach T is a living legend in the sport of wrestling, and most everyone who wrestled under him loves the man. In my opinion, the number one reason so many love him is because he has always led by developing great relationships with his athletes. Coach T is an expert at reading his athletes, and it's because he gets to know them as a person.

Now let me get something out there for you; relational leadership isn't all mushy. No, relational leadership is not soft. I mean, have you ever met my dad? He can be a scary dude. To this day if he says jump, I ask how high while I'm already in the air. And Coach T; I would never cross him. He wasn't a yeller, but the couple of times he got on to me, I listened quick, fast and in a hurry.

Relational leaders instill discipline and will kick your butt if you mess up, but they do it because they care about you as a person. The person being led also responds well because they know the leader has their best interest at heart. Maybe you've heard it said this way, "rules without relationship lead to rebellion." There is much truth to that statement. Conversely, rules with relationship lead to voluntary obedience.

Let's look at Jesus as an example of relational leadership. Jesus' disciples loved him and followed willingly because they knew He loved them back. He developed relationships with his followers and because of this they gladly followed his instructions, even when it wasn't comfortable for them. I'm certain he could have ruled with an iron fist and used his disciples as a transaction to meet his personal agenda, but that wasn't his nature or the way he chose to lead those in his charge. Jesus led relationally.

Today I encourage you to look at the game changing moves I've listed in this chapter, then decide what relational leadership would look like in your life as both a leader and follower.

GAME CHANGING MOVES:

1. Ponder the leaders (e.g. teachers, coaches, boss, etc.) in your life, both former and current, who made a lasting impact on you. Did your most impactful leaders develop a positive relationship with you and the others they led?

2. Write down some of the qualities of your favorite leaders (e.g. caring, held you to a high standard, had one-on-one talks about your vision for life, etc.)

3. How can you better develop relationships with those you lead? Write down 2-3 ideas and then put them into action this week.

MAN IN THE MIRROR

"There is a four letter word you'll never see written on a wall in graffiti, WORK."

Coach Martin Parks

I grew up in a family that believed in hard work and lived that example out daily. My dad and mom were both hard workers in every area of their lives. My dad was a teacher, coached multiple sports and ran both a lawn cutting and a painting business. My mom stayed at home to take care of us kids. She cooked full meals each evening, always had the house clean and helped every elderly woman in our neighborhood with their home. Mom and dad also cleaned local offices in the evenings to earn some extra income. They still do most of these things to this day.

When I was around seven or eight years old, I started painting with my dad from time to time. The summer before third grade I was mowing two yards in our neighborhood. By sixth grade, I had more than 20 yards of my own to mow. My dad would drop me off in a neighborhood, I'd mow a few yards while he went to whatever paint job he was currently working on, then he'd stop by later to get me and take me to the next neighborhood to cut grass. When I was finished mowing for the day, I'd help him paint.

This was my lifestyle all the way through high school and into my first couple years of college. Break time was going to a sports practice or lifting weights. Don't worry; I still had plenty of time to hang out with my friends and be a kid, but hard work was a way of life in our household.

When it came to coaching, my dad preached hard work to his football and wrestling teams. It was a staple of his programs, and all of his athletes were better because of it. Growing up in that environment melded the value of hard work into my mind.

Through these experiences, I've learned multiple lessons on hard work I believe are valuable for every person. Below are five I want to share with you today:

1. You can never get back time. When I was a young man, former athletes would stop by our house to speak with my dad, who had been their coach. After a good talk, this statement was often overheard "I wish I had worked harder when I was playing sports." My dad would always look at me when they left our house and say "Did you hear that? Don't let that be you, son. You can never gain back time. If you don't work hard today, the opportunity will be gone and you can never get it back."

2. You can't lie to the man in the mirror. A few years ago one of my assistant wrestling coaches, Frank Crosson, who is also a college football coach at Washburn University, was talking to our team. He made this statement "You can't lie to the man in the mirror. Only you know if you worked your hardest today. You can fool your coaches and teammates sometimes, but the mirror never lies. When you look yourself in the eyes, only you know if you worked your hardest, did it with integrity, and left everything you have in practice or a competition." I never forgot that statement and use it with my athletes every year.

3. The harder you work, the harder it is to surrender. This is a quote by one of the greatest coaches of all time, Vince Lombardi. As a longtime coach and athlete myself, I saw this play out time and again. Teams or individuals who work their tails off do not quit when the going gets tough. They battle because they put in work to reach their goals. They dedicate themselves and invest their hearts into their work. On the other hand, teams and individuals that cut corners, take the easy way out and cheat themselves out of hard work. When things don't go their way, they fold up and quit. Why? It's simple; they did not invest their hearts into their training nor complete the hard work necessary for success.

4. Whatever you do, work at it with all your heart, as working for the Lord, not for man. This is one of my favorite scriptures and can be found in Colossians 3:23. Hard work has great value and will help you go a long way in life, but working hard for a greater purpose is even more powerful. When you work with all your heart and you do this for the Lord, then you'll push yourself beyond what your body and mind would normally allow. When you get tired, a signal flashes in your brain and says "You represent God; you are His creation. He has given you great abilities, now use them to glorify Him!" This Scripture can and should apply to every situation in our lives. Whether we are working on something we love or doing something out of duty, it doesn't matter. Our mindset in all things should be to work hard because we are doing it for God and not just ourselves or someone else.

5. All hard work brings a profit, but mere talk leads only to poverty. This ancient wisdom comes from Proverbs 14:23 in the Bible. I love that this message is laid out plain and simple. Work hard and good things happen; slack and you get the results you deserve. In other words, be about it, don't just talk about it.

All five of these points about hard work can be applied to sports, business, parenting, marriage, etc. so today I encourage you to incorporate them into your life and never be afraid of that four letter word not written on the walls in graffiti, WORK.

GAME CHANGING MOVES:

1. In what areas of your life do you work extra hard and why?

2. In what areas of your life do you need to step up the work you put in and why?

3. Who are you really working for . . . yourself, other people, or God?

4. Read Proverbs 14:23 and Colossians 3:23. What do these scriptures have to say about work?

KEYS TO BECOMING A CHAMPION

Wrestling has long been one of my passions and a major part of my life. I attended my first wrestling match as a newborn and started participating as soon as I could walk. My dad is a National Hall of Fame wrestling coach, so I was around the sport all the time. During my wrestling career, I competed in close to a thousand matches and reached college All-American status.

Coach Martin Parks teaching his son Chad Parks a wrestling stance. (1978)

Throughout my competitive wrestling career, I had the great fortune of being trained by excellent coaches. My dad, Martin Parks, fostered in me the love and work ethic needed to succeed in wrestling and life. My private technique coach, Richard Winton, added an enormous amount of technical knowledge and mental training to my wrestling game. Then my National Hall of Fame college coach, Jody Thompson, took the potential within me and brought it into fruition.

Now I am a wrestling coach myself and have the opportunity to work with a tremendous number of excellent coaches and wrestlers. I constantly study, observe and learn what it takes to be a champion. There is no exact recipe, but there are many common disciplines champions practice daily in order to be the best.

I am going to share with you five disciplines I learned over the years and applied in my own life. These disciplines helped me achieve success in wrestling, coaching, business, etc. My hope is that these disciplines will help you become a champion in the craft of your choice as well.

1. Total commitment. Wrestling is more than a sport; it's a lifestyle. In this sport you must be all in or all out, there is no glory in the in-between.

2. Become a student of the game. If you want to become a champion wrestler, you need to constantly learn and work on perfecting your sport. This takes dedication and being intentional about study and practice, beyond what the coach demands. Extra activities such as journaling, film study, visualization, and reading books on success go a long way in helping a wrestler become a student of the game.

3. Outwork everyone. My goal has always been simple; be the hardest worker in the room. I fully believe in working smart, but you must work hard, period.

4. Surround yourself with great coaches and teammates. The best coaches make you want to battle and win for them. They push you to your mental and physical edge and then throw you over it, but thankfully they attached a bungee cord to you when you weren't looking. Your teammates should push you to be the best every day. They should inspire you, drive you and make you better.

5. Be willing to get hit in the face. Wrestling is a physical sport, and you will get hit in the face. Some people turn their heads and look away when they hand fight, take a shot or defend a shot. Others say "Forget that, I'm going to put my head in there and use it as a tool to help me get the win." I ask you to review the five disciplines in this chapter and think about them in the context of your life. These disciplines are not limited to success in wrestling; they apply to your sport, your job, your family life, etc. We all need to totally commit, constantly learn, work hard, surround ourselves with good people and be willing to get hit, yet keep on fighting through it to get some wins.

GAME CHANGING MOVES:

1. After reviewing the five disciplines outlined in this chapter, write down one or two you'd like to improve in your life.

2. Do you have great people surrounding you? You will become like the people you hang out with the most. Knowing this, do you need to find some new friends and mentors, or are you around ones who will help you reach your full potential?

3. Read 1 Corinthians 15:33 and Ecclesiastes 4:9-12. What do these Scriptures say about the importance of surrounding yourself with good people?

OUTSIDE
THE BOX

Many would say I'm an "outside the box" coach. This is because my wrestling teams use a number of uncommon techniques and have success with them on a consistent basis. We also utilize unique practice methodology that has allowed many of our wrestlers to advance quickly. When I coached football, we ran some crazy offenses which scored a lot of points each game. Yet I do not choose to coach outside the box just to do it; everything has a purpose. Though as a warning, I found choosing to work "outside the box" doesn't always make you a favorite of those who refuse to look at sports (or life) from a fresh perspective. Do it anyway!

What I know firsthand is that we all get stuck in a box from time to time in our lives. Not a real box that you use for storage, but a metaphorical box. What I mean is, many people get locked into certain patterns of thinking and therefore cannot see options that may be obvious to others.

A few years after finishing my college wrestling career, I began training in Jiu Jitsu to add to my hand-to-hand combat skills and channel some competitive energy. I wanted to take part in a sport that was similar to wrestling but also vastly different in a few areas. I felt Jiu Jitsu would complement my wrestling skill set but also fall outside the scope of my knowledge in a way that would challenge me. In addition, I wanted to learn Jiu Jitsu concepts that would hopefully expand my mind in wrestling and help me become a better coach.

During my first Jiu Jitsu practice I fell in love with what I was experiencing. My brain was racing a thousand miles per hour and taking in as much technique as possible. I remember thinking "How could I have been in grappling situations my entire life and have never seen or felt some of these positions? How did I not know that they exist?"

My mind was trapped in a box, and I didn't know what I didn't know. It's that simple.

2nd Degree Brazilian Jiu Jitsu Black Belt Mike Mrkulic & Chad Parks after training. (2010)

I continued to study and train Jiu Jitsu for years, always taking from it concepts or principles that could be crossed over into wrestling. Sure, there are many Jiu Jitsu techniques that are not legal in the sport of wrestling, but principles are principles and can cross over.

It was the recognition of these principles from different positions that allowed my mind to open up and see what it could not see before. This new recognition allowed me to escape the box that had been built from years and years of training in the same sport.

Sometimes we need something from the outside to come in and rock our world. We need a different viewpoint that can use what we may already know but in a different way. Here is the story of a simple example that happened a few years ago in my wrestling room.

We had a wrestling manager, Kirsten Pelc, who was brand new to our sport. She wanted to be a part of a school activity and decided to join the wrestling team as a manager. During her first week in the room she decided to help mop the mats after wrestling practice. We use a mat mop with a six foot wide plate at the base that holds on a mop pad via velcro. The mats are sprayed with mat cleaner and the mop is pushed forward along the mat to clean and remove any debris. This is how our wrestling team and every other wrestling team with this particular mat mop has completed the task for years and years.

Well, our novice manager didn't understand the "normal" way of cleaning mats with our mop. She started mopping and moved right along like it was nothing. We all saw what was happening, but no one wanted to hurt her feelings by telling her she was doing it incorrectly. Instead of walking behind the mop and pushing it up and down the mats, she was walking in front of the mop and dragging it behind her up and down the mats. When she finished cleaning, she put up the mop and smiled widely with pride at the job she had just completed.

I told the other coaches "Tomorrow we can show her how to mop the mats right so they get cleaned well." Then I thought about it for a moment and said "She just cleaned the mats in about half the normal time with her method, but there is no way she cleaned the mats well." I grabbed the mop, placed it on the mat and start pulling it backwards just as our new manager had done minutes before.

"What in the world? No way; there is no way."

Then I started laughing as the other coaches thought maybe I was losing my mind. I told them "Our non-wrestling manager just figured out how this mop was actually designed to be used." They asked me what I was talking about, so I showed them. You see, when you push the mop forward it causes extreme drag and makes it difficult to push. It's actually a little exhausting, to tell the truth. Plus you are walking over the area you just cleaned since the mop is in front of you. But this new "wrong" way of using the mop allows the user to keep the mop pad flat, walk with very little drag and clean your footprints as you go. It is incredibly easy and takes little effort to complete what had previously been a difficult task.

Now every time we are at a wrestling meet and see people cleaning the mats by pushing their mop forward, we all laugh and say "They just don't know the secret."

Our manager is not the first outsider to step in and change the game because she lacked the "knowledge" of the proper methods for a task. Take a look at football, and you'll find coaches who went outside the box and changed the game. I'm not talking about mopping a mat either; I mean really changed the game.

The first "outside the box" coach who comes to mind is Mike Leach, the famed founder of the "Air Raid" offense. Coach Leach is a rare breed. He did not play college football but is now one of the premier coaches in the game. He took conventional football knowledge, applied his own spin and created one of the highest scoring offensive systems ever seen in the sport. Coach Leach wasn't locked in a box mentally after years of being trained by common practice. On the contrary, he looked outside the box, changed common practice and created a system now used by others around the nation in football at every level.

Coaches like Mike Leach exist in every sport and are needed for progress to take place. Outside of sports there are many leaders who thought outside the box and changed standard practice forever. Companies such as Apple, Airbnb, Amazon, etc. were built by leaders who chose to take principles and apply them in ways the world had never seen before.

I encourage you to think outside the box in your own life. Actually, I encourage you to do more than think outside the box; I challenge you to act outside the box. This can be done in every area of your life if you sit back and think, then choose to act upon those thoughts. These actions are not always easy, and as I stated earlier, they may be frowned upon by others who are unwilling to change. Do it anyway!

GAME CHANGING MOVES:

1. Study great leaders in an area of interest that have acted outside the box. A few examples are Jesus, Steve Jobs and Mike Leach.

2. Pick one area of your life in which you'd like to experience greater success. Think about this area and see if you can find some methods outside the norm that can be applied to help you break the seal on your own mental box.

3. Realize that you can learn from everything and everyone when you become intentional about it.

4. Read John 3:1-21. How is Jesus an outside the box leader?

CONTROL THE CONTROLLABLES

"We don't have control over outcomes, but we do have control over how we use our time."
Joshua Medcalf (Author of Chop Wood, Carry Water)

We live in an outcomes based society. Our youth start school young and are driven to make straight A's from day one. Even if they attend a school that no longer uses letter grades, the focus is still on meeting or exceeding built in standards.

Athletes are motivated both internally and externally to be the best at their given sport. They are encouraged to set big goals and shoot for the stars. These goals often include winning state titles, national titles and achieving All-State or All-American status. Each of these is an outcome based goal built around what is considered winning or success.

Successful outcomes in and of themselves are awesome, and winning is fun. I believe people should dream big, have a grand vision and set the bar high at all times. The issue does not reside in wanting successful outcomes or shooting for the stars. The problem is that people often focus solely on outcomes, when in reality outcomes are beyond their control.

However, what is not beyond an individual's control is how they prepare themselves throughout their journey. As a coach I often speak to my athletes about controlling the controllables and letting go of the rest. When they heed this advice, the result usually brings about the desired outcomes anyway. For example, my wrestlers cannot control whether or not they become a state champion. What they can control is how hard they work, their off season training, highlight film study, visualization, becoming a student of the sport, eating right, getting proper rest, etc. These are what I call the controllables. Each wrestler can choose to put his time, effort and energy into the controllables or he can choose to expend those valuable resources on the uncontrollables. Time, effort, and energy will be spent either way. It is a choice.

Do not get this confused with dumbing down the vision; that is not an option in my book.

I have heard teachers and coaches tell a student "You will never be a professional athlete, just look at the statistics. It's stupid to think you will compete at that level one day, so don't waste your time." I've had coaches get mad at me for telling kids they can succeed at a high level. A good example of this is when I told one of my middle school football teams they could win a state title in high school, and a couple of adults got mad at me. They said "that's just unrealistic and too much pressure for these young kids."

Well, to say this line of thinking in adults infuriates me is an understatement. I have personally coached a player who is now in the NFL. I have coached multiple wrestling state champions, college All-Americans, and one wrestler even made it to the U.S. Olympic Trial finals, but with each of these athletes and teams, there was never a bold statement made without explaining that the outcome in and of itself is not the focus. The focus is to control everything that can be controlled in order to prepare for an opportunity at greatness.

This thought process of controlling the controllables reaches far beyond sports and into every area of our lives. Parents cannot control how their children will end up when they become adults, yet they can invest love, provide opportunity and create an environment to give their children the best possibility to one day become great adults. Business leaders cannot control the financial success of their company, but they can control who they hire, how they develop those employees and the decisions that will nurture growth for the individuals under their care.

Ultimately, focusing on outcomes is a waste of our time, effort and energy. Focusing on outcomes means we are attempting to control the uncontrollables. On the contrary, when the focus is placed upon our preparation, then we are giving life to those areas we can control. This intentional focus upon the controllables allows us to fully develop and possibly shoot past the outcomes we desired in the first place. Controlling the controllables does not guarantee success, but it does place you in a position of knowing you've done everything possible to succeed. That preparation process in and of itself is a win in life, no matter the area of focus.

GAME CHANGING MOVES:

1. Take a quick inventory of your life and write down any areas where you have been placing your time, effort and energy into uncontrollables.

2. Now write down 3-5 concrete items you can control, and make a decision to place your focus on those items.

3. Where can you improve your preparation in a given area (sports, leadership, parenting, etc.) that will give you the greatest chance of reaching a desired outcome?

4. Read the parable of the talents in Matthew 25:14-30. Notice that two of the servants got into action right away and focused on what they could control. The last servant was so worried about the outcome (not upsetting the master) that he placed his focus on the uncontrollables, and the result was not a favorable one.

BUTTERFLIES

Excitement, nerves, butterflies! Make it stop; give me more; make it stop; give me more... ahhhh! I don't know if this is horrible or if it's awesome.

If you have ever competed in a sport, performed in front of people, spoken to a large crowd or taken part in something really important to you, then you know about that feeling in the pit of your stomach. You know about nerves and those often-dreaded butterflies.

Since my dad is a long-time wrestling coach, I have wrestled since I could walk. Overall, I've probably competed in close to 1000 matches when combining folkstyle wrestling, freestyle wrestling and Greco-Roman wrestling. I have also competed in Jiu-Jitsu matches as well.

Guess what? I was nervous every single time I competed in these matches. You'd think I'd get used to it right? Wrong.

I also coached wrestling for years. First at the college level, and then at the high school level. Along with this, I was a middle school football coach for 13 years, and have been in the corner for many Professional MMA fighters (basically the coach in the corner), and a lot of these fights have been on major shows.

I still get nervous and the butterflies start forming a speedway in my stomach when my guys compete. To be honest, it's often worse than when I was competing myself. Actually, it's the reason I decided to write about this particular topic.

What I'm getting at here is the fact that I have competed a lot and been around tons of competition, and I still get nervous. How do I deal with the nerves in competition? How does this apply to everyday real life?

My philosophy over the years continues to evolve. Many influences shaped and formed this philosophy into what it is today. So, let me tell you a couple stories that really stand out in my mind which have helped form my philosophy.

I was a senior at Pawhuska High School and warming up for the finals of our home wrestling tournament, the Carman Classic. While warming-up, wrestling legend and Olympic champion Doug Blubaugh comes over and places his hands on my shoulders and starts talking to me.

Doug: "You nervous?"

Me: "Yes, sir."

Doug: "Good."

Here is what is going through my mind: "Wait what? Good, what does he mean 'good'? Don't nerves show weakness? Nerves mean I'm scared, right?"

But Doug said, "Nerves mean you care about the sport son. The day you lose those butterflies, it's time to get out. You are nervous because it means something to you and that's good. Let that fuel you."

This conversation changed my perspective on feeling nervous. I went from having a negative perspective on nerves to realizing they aren't bad. Nerves mean I care, and caring is a good thing in my book.

As a side note, I tech falled my guy in the finals. I mean come on, Doug Blubaugh warmed me up and was sitting next to my dad in the corner coaching me. That poor kid had no chance against me in that match.

The next story that helped shape my philosophy about nerves is from 1998. I was in the semi-finals of a college wrestling tourney, and my coach (Hall of Famer Jody Thompson aka Coach T) walks up and hands me a couple jelly beans. "They'll give you some energy, eat 'em." Coach T always did things like that in serious moments. Then Coach T makes this statement "You know, nerves are a good thing. They are your body's way of preparing for battle. They make you faster, stronger and maybe even a little smarter. Nerves are your warrior instinct kicking into gear. You are a warrior!" Wow! What a way to look at nerves! Now those butterflies aren't here to make me feel scared and sick. They are here to make me faster, stronger and smarter. I can take that!

The last story is short and these words come from God Himself! While reading through the Bible one day, I ran across this Scripture:

"Don't worry about anything; instead, pray about everything. Tell God what you need, and thank him for all he has done. Then you will experience God's peace, which exceeds anything we can understand. His peace will guard your hearts and minds as you live in Christ Jesus." Philippians 4:6-7

These words spoke to me, and I memorized them that day. I remembered these words when feeling nervous, and they always calm my spirit. I recited this Scripture before many wrestling matches, and I recite it today when I feel overwhelmed or nervous about anything.

So, how do these stories and sage advice apply to real life? Good question!

First, let me point out that perspective goes a long way. A change in perspective can turn the seemingly bad into good, which can change your life in so many ways.

Second, many of the issues we deal with in sports also apply to life. Let me quote Coach Jody Thompson to make this point. These are a few of the thoughts he sent me in an email as we were talking just last week.

"Having a deep philosophy on dealing with nerves is important. This philosophy is one that will see you through wrestling, coaching, and life.... because it's all the same. Everyday life can wear you down.... just think of the myriad things your environment plunks down on you. Often we humans just need a little bump up to keep us from drowning in the complications we face."

You see, life is full of moments and situations that can bring on those butterflies. These situations can be good or bad, but either way they exist. Since this is a fact, then it's a good idea to have the correct perspective in order to deal with them in the proper manner.

In summation, here is what I believe about nerves and butterflies. They are a good thing and mean that you care. They are a feeling preparing you to be faster, stronger and smarter when the need is there. Pray when you feel this way and God will give you peace and a calm spirit in the storm!

My hope is that these stories and overall philosophy help you deal with butterflies as they helped me.

GAME CHANGING MOVES:

1. In what areas of your life do you have to deal with butterflies?

2. How have you dealt with them in the past and how has that worked out for you?

3. Which story in this chapter hit home for you and has brought clarity on how to deal with or utilize butterflies?

4. Write down Philippians 4:6-7 on a note card and memorize it. This scripture is powerful and great to say aloud when you need it, especially in dealing with butterflies.

DEAL WITH PRESSURE

If you are reading this, then I assume you are alive. If you are alive, then you know something about feeling pressure. Pressure in sports, pressure at home, pressure on the job, etc. If you have felt pressure or feel it daily, then it might benefit you to look at it from a different perspective.

In the last chapter I spoke about ways to handle nerves and butterflies, which are closely related to pressure. Before I get into dealing with pressure, let's take a close look at one definition of it. Pressure: "A burdensome condition that is hard to bear." Ouch. That's uncomfortable just in definition alone. None of us want burdens that are hard to bear, but that's what pressure is and it's not enjoyable.

Since I coach and also think of myself as an athlete, I will talk about pressure using sports as the prime example.

I am a coach's son, so I know a thing or two about pressure. My dad is not just any coach either; he is a coach who has been inducted into the National Wrestling Hall of Fame. Needless to say, I had a few expectations hanging on me every time I walked onto a wrestling mat.

Hey, at least I'm not James, Jesus' brother. Can you imagine the pressure James felt at a wedding when Jesus wasn't around and the wine ran out? I wonder if Mary ever asked "James, why can't you be more like your brother Jesus?"

Being a coach's son was awesome, but it also brought added pressure, at least in my mind. Really though, all athletes feel pressure when they compete. Wrestling especially brings pressure as it is one on one, under the lights, no place to hide and no one in which to blame anything.

So, how does one deal with pressure in wrestling? How does one deal with pressure in life? Good question, and I hope some of the following information will help enlighten you and change your perspective on pressure.

Shawnee Heights High School State Finalist Brett Yeagley and Coach Chad Parks talking before the State Finals in Wichita, KS. (2016)

Growing up I attended a lot of football and wrestling practices. Not just the ones I was involved in, but all the practices my dad was running for his teams. This means I got to hear and see a lot of good coaching over a number of years. It never failed that my dad would give his teams the following illustration at least one time per season, sometimes more if needed.

My dad would always say "How many of you guys have played backyard football and made incredible plays? I mean laying out for a catch and palming it with one hand or running and juking the other guy out of his socks!"

Most of the guys would raise their hand and smiles would cover their faces. Then my dad would ask "Why is it that you can make these incredible plays in backyard football?"

Silence (crickets chirping) ....

"I'll tell you why; because you are relaxed. You are out there having fun, and there is no pressure. Since there is no pressure, you open up and really use your athletic ability."

"Now, what if you always played like that? I mean you relaxed, had fun, and really used your athletic ability on Friday night? How good could you be?"

Think about this and how much truth it contains. This illustration doesn't just apply to football either. I see wrestlers look like a million bucks in practice all the time. They open up, have fun, hit sweet moves and wrestle awesome. Then they get in a match, the pressure gets to them and they are not so awesome.

What's the point here? Athletes must learn how to control their "warrior state" when going into competition. In that state they are faster, stronger and smarter, but they must also stay relaxed and have fun. In essence, play backyard football in super speed! Here is another thought on pressure two incredible programs use with their athletes. Have fun and keep it playful! Cael Sanderson and his national champion Penn State wrestling team use this philosophy in their room. Cael knows a lot about pressure as he is the only NCAA D1 wrestler to ever finish his college career undefeated. He teaches his wrestlers to have fun, keep it playful and be creative when wrestling. He says that's the best way to handle pressure on the mats.

The other major program that uses the philosophy of keep it playful is the Gracie Academy, founded by the legendary Helio Gracie.

The Gracies are the best Jiu-Jitsu practitioners and instructors in the world. These guys can take care of business in competition, business and life, but they always try to keep it playful knowing this eliminates pressure and allows for great performances.

One more thought on dealing with pressure, especially in sports, is this: there is no pressure. Yep, you heard me right; there is no pressure. This line of thought came from listening to four-time NCAA Champion Kyle Dake in an interview. He was talking about how he dealt with pressure as an elite college athlete and now as a Team USA Wrestling star. His philosophy, when added to my own, led me to this thought for athletes. At the end of the day, win or lose, your mom and dad will still love you. Your coaches will still be your coaches and care about you. You will still show up on Monday and work your tail off to achieve your goals. So really, there is no pressure.

What does exist is the hard to bear burden you place upon yourself because of the wrong perspective. This mental burden you place upon yourself has a name, and it is called pressure.

Now I want you to think about the sports examples listed above and apply them to your everyday life. Where are the areas you feel pressure? Work, your marriage, raising children, etc. What if you applied some of the information presented in this chapter to your own life? How would it help you deal with the burdens you are bearing today?

What if you relax, have fun and really use your God given abilities? What if you take care of business, but keep it playful in the midst of the process? How would it change your outlook if you realized that whether it's a good day or bad day, your wife, children and family will still love you?

Life has plenty of ups and downs, and obstacles are thrown into our pathway. These things can sometimes feel overwhelming and create a ton of pressure, but the right perspective can relieve those feelings and help you see the silver lining. This in turn can help you enjoy life and perform your best in sports, work, at home, etc. Finally, and in my mind, most important; never leave God out of the equation. I've heard my dad and my college coach, Jody Thompson, say this many times and I believe it 100 percent. All the other ideas work better when God is sought after first.

Jesus said, *"My yoke is easy to bear and the burden I give you is light."*
Matthew 11:30

I hope this helps some of you change your perspective on pressure.

GAME CHANGING MOVES:

1. Write down the areas in your life where pressure tends to overwhelm you.

2. Write down 2-3 strategies from this chapter you can apply to the pressure situations in your life.

3. Read James 1:3-13. What do these scriptures teach about pressure from the Biblical perspective?

BACK IT DOWN

I love hype sporting events. If you've ever been to the Oklahoma University vs Texas Red River Rivalry football game or attended an Oklahoma State vs Iowa wrestling dual meet, then you have experienced a hype sporting event firsthand. How about watching a UFC fight that has been built up by the marketing machine for the last six months? Even non-MMA fans get excited for matchups like that. However, all the buildup and excitement is for the fans and cannot be internalized by the athletes or their coaches.

Let me tell you about a sporting experience that changed the way I approach big events both as an athlete and now as a coach.

I was in high school and preparing to do battle in the finals of a big wrestling tournament. I would be competing against a very formidable foe for the title and was excited to do so, but long before my match had gotten underway, I was jacked sideways with emotion. My teammate and daily workout partner, Chris Walker, was also in the finals and his match was directly before mine. He was wrestling one of his biggest rivals in the finals, and we all knew it was a huge matchup. As these two mat warriors jockeyed back and forth, I was yelling with excitement and attempting to will my teammate as much strength as possible. In the end, he wrestled great and pulled out the win against his staunch rival.

As I walked onto the mat for my match, I felt pumped, focused and ready to win a title. Just a minute into the match though, I became tired, drained and confused. I mean, I was in great shape and confident in every aspect of my game so why was I already worn down?

It's simple; I was emotionally drained, and that in turn took a physical toll on my body. I ended up winning the match, but everything about it seemed difficult. When the match was over, I reflected on the day's events and decided I must make a change in my mindset concerning big events. The change took place and my new mindset was used throughout my college wrestling career. I still use and teach it as a coach.

So, what new mindset did I take on concerning big events? I learned to back it down. In other words, I learned to relax before big events instead of the natural tendency to get all pumped up before the action starts. As a long time athlete and coach, I can assure you that is not the norm.

So, what is the norm? It looks a little something like this: Athletes listening to rap or rock music on their headphones, walking back and forth getting themselves worked into a frenzy. Soon after, coaches take the athletes and give them the motivational speech of the decade. Then, athletes are filled with enough adrenaline to run through a wall. That same adrenaline has the power to zap the athletes when it's too much too soon, though; the problem is that big events are already big. There is no need to make them any grander than they already are at this point. Believe me, it's not difficult to get up mentally and physically for a big match or game.

As a coach, I work with my athletes on achieving a calm before the storm. I teach them to control what I like to call their "warrior state" so it can be unleashed with full force when the right time comes. This can be accomplished with breathing techniques, relaxing music, prayer, visualization, meditation, etc. Each athlete needs to practice and figure out what works for him before a game or meet.

Coaches Chad Parks, Jeff Albers and James Laster helping wrestler Aspen Kmiec back it down before a big match. (2011)

This skill set is extremely important in sports, but it extends beyond athletics. In life, we all face big events. It may be an interview, giving a speech, the birth of a child, etc. Life is full of big events and approaching them with the correct mindset can make a world of difference.

As a footnote, I wrestled that same foe from the finals about a month after our first match, but this time with a different mindset. The second time around I pinned him in the first period and felt on top of my game from the onset of the match. For me, that's what really drove home this new mindset and made it stick.

GAME CHANGING MOVES:

1. Read the book *An Impractical Guide To Becoming A Transformational Leader*. There is an excellent chapter called "No Hype Needed" within the book on the very topic discussed here.

2. Read Matthew 8:23-27. How do the disciples act in the midst of a storm versus the actions of Jesus?

3. Read Psalm 23:4.

THE BIG SHOW

Every sporting event has what I like to call "the big show." This is the end of the season championship event, and it's usually a high priority for teams and athletes alike. The big show is a major reason we spend a season, a year, or half a lifetime preparing to compete at the highest level in our given sport. We all want an opportunity to take part in "the big show."

That being said, what I really want to discuss is not so much the big show as it is the mindset of the athletes, coaches, parents and fans attending the event.

Now is a good time to mention that as a coach I always feel a little conflicted going into the big show for two reasons. First, this will be the last time this exact team will compete together. Second, this will be the last time our seniors will compete for our team. These facts can heighten emotions in an environment where emotions are already stimulated to the max.

The big show doesn't only affect the athlete and coach; it can bring about a roller-coaster of emotions for all involved. During these events, you may experience the highest of highs and lowest of lows, but I hope you get more highs than lows. You will see dreams crushed and dreams fulfilled during championship events. Incredible athletes will sit defeated and crying from emotional pain, while others will jump into the stands victorious to hug theirs mothers... a moment of pure joy!

Shawnee Heights High School State Champion Tyson Toelkes hugging his Mother Jenna Henderson after winning the state championship his senior season. Also pictured are Coach Derek Holly, Coach Jeff Albers and wrestler Carter Hall.

In the midst of all this chaos and bliss, I have found a simple perspective that can change this entire experience for the better. We, the coaching staff, have implemented this perspective with our athletes the last couple of seasons, and I try to keep it at the forefront of my mind as well. Do you want to know this secret perspective? Here it is. Enjoy every moment. Too simple and cliché, right? Let me give you an example of this perspective in action. I tell our wrestlers, "Enjoy every moment of the state tourney. This is the pinnacle of our sport, and you need to enjoy it. You have an opportunity to fail and an equal opportunity to succeed. Either way, be thankful for the opportunity because not everyone gets this experience. Enjoy the hotel, the warm-up, every second of every match, the fans in the stands, etc. Really take the time to mentally enjoy every part of this experience." I believe this allows our wrestlers to relieve some of the pressure on their shoulders and ultimately perform at the top of their ability level. They no longer worry about the final outcome, which is not controllable anyway. Rather they live in the moment and take everything one step at a time. They place their focus on enjoying all their sport has to offer them as athletes and human beings. Those are things they can control and focus on mentally.

As a coach, I work to have the same perspective I'm teaching my athletes during the big show. Win or lose, I come with the mindset that I'm going to enjoy the opportunity to coach each of my athletes and my team. I am going to be grateful for each second I get with them and enjoy it to the fullest. I am going to enjoy coaching with a great coaching staff that has worked hard.

Now let me throw in a side note. I'm not a robot, and emotions sometimes get the best of me. It's worth mentioning I also enjoy winning way more than losing; losing isn't fun. That being said, focusing on enjoying each moment regardless of the outcome has made coaching more enjoyable all around. It has allowed me to really appreciate the limited time I get with my athletes during their wrestling careers. Especially during our end of the season championship tournament. We only get four chances to experience this tournament, so we better make the most of each opportunity!

There it is, a simple yet profoundly powerful perspective to the big show that can transform your experience for the better. If you are an athlete, coach, parent or fan, this perspective can be utilized during your end of the season event. Actually, it goes much further than the event. This perspective can be practiced and carried over into every aspect of your life. I encourage you to enjoy each moment to the fullest extent possible.

This is life and just like in the big show, you will at some point experience the highest of the highs and the lowest of the lows. Your perspective in these moments will either improve the experience or make it worse. Choose today to enjoy each moment, and do your best to live this life full of pure joy!

GAME CHANGING MOVES:

1. Write down the following statement and then read it aloud throughout the week: I will enjoy every moment of this week and this event. I will control the controllables and let go of the rest. The hay is in the barn; now it's time to have fun!

2. Tell your athletes, coaches, parents, etc. you love them and appreciate all their support throughout the season.

3. Relax and think about more than just the big event coming up this week. Placing mental energy into worry will drain your mind and body. So have fun with family, friends and teammates in order to be your best when your best is needed.

4. Read Philippians 4:13, Proverbs 3:5, and Proverbs 18:10. Realize God has your back and all you have to do is enjoy the moment.

EMBRACE
THE MOMENT

As a lifelong athlete, I've trained and competed more than the average person. This allowed me to understand that competitive athletes are always training and looking toward the moment they get to participate in live competition. They prepare rigorously for the opportunity to test themselves in the heat of battle.

Coaches are no different, except they aren't the ones actually competing. Even still, coaches are helping athletes train and prepare for the moment they get to lay it on the line and shine. Hour upon hour is spent working on technique, developing skill, imparting strategy and improving the athlete's level of conditioning. This is all done in preparation for the moment the lights come on and the action commences.

In life beyond the ball fields, mats and courts, we spend our lives waiting for the moment in one way or another. This might be the moment we graduate, get married, have a child, or get the big promotion at work. It seems as if our lives are spent in constant preparation for these special moments.

What I want us to consider is the possibility that we may be missing the moment by waiting for and overly anticipating the moment. What does that mean?

You see, life is full of numerous moments, many of which are awesome. These special moments often happen when we are not looking for them to occur in the everyday humdrum of life. If we are to enjoy them, then we must be vigilant and intentional in looking for them.

In this vein, I tell my athletes, "We must enjoy the journey and embrace the process. Yes, we want to see our hard work pay off and the vision fulfilled, but the journey is just as important." The journey is the daily grind, and it encompasses all the moments, big and small. It is ultimately the process we go through on a daily basis that adds up over time, hopefully leading to a desired outcome. Yet the outcome is only one little piece of the puzzle. It's all the moments leading up to the outcome that end up providing the greatest source of fulfillment.

Today I challenge you to not only wait on the big moments in life, but to also live in the moment right now. Enjoy every step of your journey and realize that you are in fact living out some of life's greatest moments. Don't let your life pass you by waiting on the moment, only to miss it many times over.

GAME CHANGING MOVES:

1. Write down 2-3 good moments that happened in your life today.

2. Repeat this action over the next five days.

3. At the end of day five, look back over your good moments list and realize how blessed you are right now in your life.

4. Read 1 Thessalonians 5:18, Ephesians 5:20, and James 1:17. Let God know how thankful you are for all the moments in your life today, both big and small.

WHO IS IN
YOUR CORNER

I have a lot of experience sitting at the corner of a mat and coaching wrestlers. I've also had the privilege of sitting outside a cage and cornering some incredible mixed martial arts athletes over the years. The athletes themselves are the ones who prepared to the best of their ability and then laid it on the line in competition, but the people in their corner make a big difference as well.

Coaches Justin Vest and Chad Parks instruct Shawnee Heights High School wrestler Damon Ward.

Many times I have pondered the role of the coach/cornerman and broken down what contributes to the success or lack thereof for their athletes. I am not talking about practice or the preparation of the athlete ahead of the competition. What I am talking about is the role of the coach/cornerman once the athlete is actually in the test. I mean, the hay is in the barn at that point as far as training goes. So how does the coach/cornerman contribute when the athlete is in live action?

That is indeed a grand question and one of the reasons I've included it in this book. Below I have chosen five key elements to focus on in answering the question.

5 WAYS THE COACH/CORNERMAN CONTRIBUTES TO THE SUCCESS OF THEIR ATHLETE

1. Provide Confidence. Have you ever been around someone who made you feel confident? I have had a few coaches in my day who made me feel that way. I can't really nail it down or explain it either, but what I can tell you is that I'd run through a wall for them, and they made me feel like I could do it too. I've also been around certain friends who gave me the same feeling and it's awesome. That's what a good coach/cornerman provides for his athletes. He gives them a confidence that allows them to compete at a higher level than they would have alone.

2. Deliver Instruction. Good coaches/cornermen know how to deliver timely instruction to their athletes in the heat of the battle. They know the sport, they know the athlete and they make their words count. Their banter is deliberate and full of useful information that allows the athlete to see beyond his own limitations in the midst of organized chaos.

3. Administer Encouragement. Anyone can be negative and state what a person is doing wrong. As a matter of fact, I believe some people have advanced degrees in fault finding, but a good coach/

cornerman knows how and when to encourage an athlete. They understand how to motivate the athlete through encouragement and draw forth a level of "heart" that even the athlete didn't know they possessed.

4. Tell it like it is. A good coach/cornerman is encouraging, but they also know when to tell it like it is. They don't sugarcoat a situation just to make the athlete feel good inside. They lay out the facts and then provide solutions. That's right; they provide solutions after telling it like it is. Side note: I feel strongly about this issue. Don't present a problem unless you can present some solutions. Otherwise you are just complaining. For example, if I have an athlete that keeps gassing out (getting tired) in competition, I don't tell him it's okay because gassing out isn't important. I also don't tell him to get in better shape and then walk away. No, I will address the issue and then dissect that athlete's training habits, eating habits, pre-competition warm-up, etc. When I have narrowed down the problem, then I will provide a solution to help fix the problem.

5. Be there win or lose. Good coaches/cornermen will be there for their athlete, win or lose. They don't just hang around when the athlete is sitting at star status and then bail out when things go bad. Emotions can run high on wins and low on losses. Cool down periods are needed either way, but at the end of the day, a real coach/cornerman will be there to celebrate or even cry with his athlete. Do you know what I love about all five of these points? They all apply to life. Yep, these aren't just for the athlete and coach/cornerman. These five points are for each of us. We each need to have someone in our corner that provides us with confidence, delivers instruction, administers encouragement, tells it like it is, and will be there for us win or lose.

So my question for you is this... *who is in your corner?*

GAME CHANGING MOVES:

1. Who do you know that makes you feel confident every time you are around them or talk to them on the phone? Call that person today and let them know how they make you feel and that you appreciate them.

2. Make a list of qualities you believe make up a good coach/cornerman. Now ask yourself if you are living out these qualities.

3. Read Proverbs 12:15 and Proverbs 17:17. What does this ancient wisdom have to say about taking advice and helping people?

THE FOUR INTANGIBLES

The next two chapters are what I'll call inspiration for both you and me. They are game changing moves written by two of the best coaches and mentors I know. I asked these two men to provide me with what they consider to be a game changing move for both sports and life. Each man penned me a letter full of wisdom that I will share with you in this chapter and the next.

This chapter provides insight from National Hall of Fame wrestling coach Martin Parks, who also happens to be my dad. Coach Parks has coached wrestling for over 30 years in the state of Oklahoma. He has achieved tremendous success as a wrestling coach, football coach, teacher and school administrator. Coach Parks is known and loved by many for his ability to teach, train and inspire. His heart is huge, and he puts it into everything he does in life.

In my 30 plus years as a wrestling coach, I have witnessed the athlete with greater ability defeated by the athlete with lesser ability. I have heard many coaches state "I just do not understand how this happens," and I have been included in this group too.

Many times, I have personally witnessed the average athlete move forward because they simply placed four intangibles in their lives. I want you to know, no coach can give you these four intangibles—it is a matter of personal choice.

Below are four intangible qualities that can allow the average athlete to succeed and even flourish, but this information can be applied by anyone to help them succeed in athletics, parenting, or business.

1) **Work Ethic** – You must be driven to improve day by day. You have to study film on your own, analyze technique, work on your endurance and do it all because you want to improve.

2) **Coachable** - You need to be willing to listen, make changes and adapt. Remember this is a personal choice. The coach can offer his wisdom, but it's up to you to make the changes.

3) **Effort** - Dan Gable states "My style has always been one of aggressive behavior. No matter if I win or lose—I am coming after you. The more I am in on your legs—the less you are in on mine." This is a great example of possessing a willingness to put forth effort on a continual basis.

4) **Heart** - Have you ever watched someone just give up? Have you ever watched someone pull out a win against a better athlete because they just refused to lose? Choose to have a courageous heart. Let me remind you; no coach, parent or friend can give you any of these four intangibles. You must make the choice with your own heart and mind.

Why?

I believe God made it that way on purpose. We as coaches can help you along the journey, but when the journey is over, only you will know in your own mind and heart if you had and practiced the four intangibles. Did you have work ethic, were you coachable or were you the know it all unwilling to make changes; did you give great effort in practice and during the matches, and did you ever just reach down and pull from your own heart win or lose? Coaches, parents, bosses and mentors can each guide and support, but it's ultimately up to an individual to employ the four intangibles in their own life.

Lastly, you can see the results of these four intangibles, but you cannot touch them, buy them or go get one of them off the shelf. They must be taught and then put into action, which is up to you.

GAME CHANGING MOVES:

1. Read through the four intangibles. Do you see one or more you need to work on starting today?

2. Who is responsible for implementing the four intangibles that lead to success?

3. Which of the four intangibles do you find most important and why?

4. Read Judges 7. What example does Gideon provide for us that relates to the four intangibles?

THE SUCCESS
RATIO

The wisdom in this chapter was shared with me by my college wrestling coach Jody Thompson. Coach Thompson, coached wrestling for 38 years on both the high school and collegiate levels and has been inducted into the College Wrestling National Hall of Fame. He spent the majority of his coaching years building NJCAA Wrestling Powerhouse Labette Community College in Parsons, KS. Coach Thompson achieved tremendous success as a college and international wrestler, college wrestling coach, college professor and college athletic director and is a legend in the wrestling world. What's even more important and impressive is the fact that he impacted thousands upon thousands of lives in a positive manner through his uncanny ability to connect and motivate people to become the best version of themselves. The following words were provided by Coach Thompson, and I'm certain will inspire you as they inspired me.

One often hears about how participating in competitive athletics during an individual's life will provide an advantage to that individual's success ratio throughout their life, but is it the participation itself or the lessons learned?

Dealing with the severity that life throws against you can be traumatic and life altering. Over these many years as an instructor and coach, I have often offered up to my teams the realization that life's not fair, is not always happy, and there is no guarantee that your own personal "happily ever after" will exist. Much of life is full of adversity that may include debts, deception, disease, wars, firings, arguments, divorce, feuds, disappointments, death, bad traffic and oh yes, taxes. Thus, the old saying, "never promised you a rose garden," is an actuality. Life is a constant struggle. It is up to you, not life, to decide whether you are happy.

Indeed, there is much to be said about the attributes one can garner from athletic participation: teamwork, determination, confidence, focus, industry, competitiveness, planning, attitude, synergy, adversity, bouncing back after failure, handling the headiness of success and etc.

I once read an interesting article that made me think about those attributes in a different light. The article outlined a persuasive argument that competitive sports do not create but rather 'stimulate and develop' positive integral attributes already innate and possessed by the individual. If one were to accept this philosophy, it could be pointed out that by just merely being in a sport one gets to practice using these skills on a daily basis. I suggest no sport exemplifies the aforementioned attributes better than the sport of wrestling.

Coach Chad Parks, wrestler Barrett Stickelman, and National Hall of Fame Coach Jody Thompson. (2016)

The lessons that exist in wrestling can be pointed out in abundance. They lurk in practice, a challenge match or should the athlete claw his way into the finals of a tournament, the failure of an incompetent official to award points correctly. Most athletes are taught to rise above a loss, to work with their team, to listen to the coach, to train in-season and out, to eat properly and to be a good sport. In wrestling, there are the added factors of cutting weight, the risk of failure while alone and facing opponents in front of fans, family and friends, as well as the 'no-excuse rule,' which is that you cannot blame a teammate for your loss or that your opponent was taller or bigger than you.

In addition, I would offer up it is the wrestler who is 'not' a natural athlete who benefits most from being in the sport. For one thing, they have to work harder. Some wrestlers are naturally stronger and faster and any sport comes easily to them. The non-athlete pays a bigger price to reap similar benefits. When you invest so much into what you are doing you learn more from the process, whatever the outcome. This is a prime example of the thought that the journey is more important than the destination, for what is learned through the grind and hard work builds the character that defines the person.

Finally, I believe a sport in and of itself does not teach an athlete life lessons. The lessons lie within the opportunities provided by the sport and must be pointed out by people such as coaches, athletes, or parents. Once revealed, the lessons can be seen and focused upon by the athlete and then used in multiple areas of life, thus increasing the success ratio.

GAME CHANGING MOVES:

1. In what area of your life have you not been a natural and were forced to work extra hard to succeed? What did you learn from the bonus work you put in?

2. Write down a time life sent a storm your way but you came out stronger on the other side.

3. Read 1 Corinthians 12:14-16. What does this scripture teach us about teamwork and the importance of each individual?

HOW WE WENT 133-35 IN FOOTBALL

Wrestling is my number one sport, but I am passionate about football as well. My dad was a football coach for close to 30 years, so I was around it a lot growing up. After graduating from college, I jumped right in as a head middle school football coach and soon discovered a passion for coaching this great American sport.

Admittedly, I am not as knowledgeable about football as I am wrestling, but I do know more about pigskin than the average person and have a knack for this whole coaching thing. After 12 years of being a head middle school football coach, I decided to hang up the whistle and focus my time and energy in other areas. That being said, I want share some actions and lessons that allowed my teams to accumulate an overall record of 133-35 in 12 years (this is A team and B team combined). These lessons apply to football, but more importantly, they apply to life.

1. Passion- *"Nobody cares how much you know until they know how much you care."* - President Theodore Roosevelt.

My coaching staff cares about our athletes, and our athletes know it. If you want to push your athletes toward greatness and get them to respond positively, then you better care about them.

2. Develop a Purpose- Why are we coaching this team? What are our goals this season for the individuals on the team? As a coaching staff, we show up every day to win. I like to win; it's fun. Losing is not fun, and it is not motivating, but you may not win everything every day and this is a life lesson. Therefore, we must have a purpose deeper than just winning games and a focus on the process.

3. Everything is on purpose- Why waste time? Practice planning, game planning, game execution, etc. Every facet of the game should be broken down and the most efficient plans then put into place.

4. Think outside the box- This is a passion of mine. Those who have been around my football program or wrestling program know I not only think outside the box but that for me the box doesn't exist. As a coaching staff, we have been flexible and looked for ways to succeed that might not be the norm. I love coaches like Chip Kelly, Mike Leach and Kevin Kelley. These guys are not afraid to break the mold and get creative. Most coaches coach how they were coached. They do what their coaches did and don't stray far off that pathway. This is fine if your coach or maybe your coaching mentor was awesome. If this is the case, take their awesomeness and implement it into your program. Believe me, I take what I have learned from great coaches and run with it. No need to totally reinvent the wheel in every area, but football, like all sports, is dynamic. The game changes, the kids change, and coaches must therefore change. By the way, I'm not saying to abandon the basics, but maybe re-think how you teach them.

5. Be flexible- Being flexible is related to thinking outside the box, in my mind. Each season we run a little different offense and defense than the season before. Why would we do something crazy like that? It's simple. Each team has different kids with different skills. We may run a system similar to the season before, but we always make the necessary adjustments in order to bring out the best in each team.

6. Keep it simple- Sports in general are complex. Football is complex, but we often make it more complex than it needs to be. Our coaching staff has tried to identify ways to teach it so that kids can "get it." We do not cut corners as I believe details are vital. Details can take a player from average to good, good to great, and great to exceptional, but how you teach and implement the details doesn't have to be super complex. A number of years ago we developed a simple system of hand signals for our offense and defense. This is not a novel idea, but we were the first middle school to do this in our area. These signals allow us to run a no huddle offense and defense. We can therefore play with speed, like the big boys do. These hand signals look complicated to the untrained eye, but they really are simple. We can use the hand signals for any offense or defense we choose to implement in a season. Oh yeah, we don't have a playbook either. We have hand signal sheets. Once you learn the system, the playbook is literally endless. The coaches are the ones who have to think fast in this system, allowing the athletes to slow down their game mentally.

7. Keep it fun- Football season can get long, drawn out and beat you up. That's why we work super hard but also have fun. Each week we add new plays to keep our athlete's minds stimulated. Some of these plays are crazy. I love a good trick play! I know our opposing coaches work on defending some of the plays we "trick" them with each season. We have run a few so tricky that even the officials had no idea where the ball was until we started yelling "Go, Go, Go" as our player ran through open space and into the end zone. I have a huge smile on my face right now just thinking about it; oh, so sweet! We also scrimmage a lot during practice. Nothing allows a young player to learn better than drills and then getting to use their new skills. This allows us coaches to make adjustments and take advantage of teaching opportunities during practice. Again, this is fun for the athletes and fun for us coaches.

8. High expectations- We walk into every season expecting to go 7-0 on both the A and B teams (14-0 for the season). It doesn't always happen, but we expect it to and this helps build a great culture. Our players know from day one that they will work hard, be pushed to their limits, compete every single practice and also become students of the game. Setting high expectations has allowed us to take many teams and play above their actual skill level. It has allowed us to teach players about heart, grit, and mental toughness and has allowed us coaches to be encouragers and believe in our players until they believed in themselves.

9. Real life application- All sports should relate to life. When we coach our football players, we strive to teach them as much about the game as we can in a nine or ten-week season. We also strive to teach them lessons through football that relate to real life, including: the value of teamwork, personal responsibility, hard work, grit, having fun, being your brother's keeper, taking care of business and love. Nine or ten weeks may not be that long, but I'm willing to bet that in 9 or 10 weeks we have changed some lives for the better.

10. The Stud- One good running back at the middle school level can win most games for you or kick your butt. The game is about more than just one good player, but I'm telling you from experience, one good running back is a game changer.

GAME CHANGING MOVES:

1. Which of these ten lessons stands out to you the most and why?

2. Write down 3-5 lessons you have learned from your favorite sport or activity.

3. Who are the coaches, teachers, or leaders that made you love a sport, subject or job? Write down their names and take a trip down memory lane.

4. Read Philippians 3:13-16. In football we want to cross the goal line and score points, but what is the ultimate goal as explained in these verses?

GOOD
TO GREAT

Recently one of my mentors, Corby Stickelman, and his wife Sherry decided it was time for a change in their lives. It was time for a greater challenge that could fulfill the calling God had placed before them. They felt a pull upon their hearts and a stirring in their souls that refused to be suppressed. This awesome couple heard a still small voice prompting them forward and telling them to grow. So, what did they do?

My friends sold their home, moved their family to a different state and embraced a new challenge head on. Wow, that's awesome and scary.

You see, my mentor and his family were doing great. Their home life, church, business, school, etc. was all going exceptionally well. God had blessed them greatly. So why the change?

Here's why…

They knew in their hearts they were not called to just exist in this life. They were not called to reach a certain level of comfort and then coast. This couple knew that to whom much is given, much is expected. They understood that they must answer God's call with a heart full of faith and expectancy in order to become all He desires for them to be in this life.

So why am I sharing this story? I'm sharing it because we can each learn a few lessons from my dear friends. Okay, don't freak out. I'm not telling you to sell your house and move to another state. What I am telling you is that we can all learn and then apply what we've learned to our own unique life circumstances.

The overarching lessons are as follows:

1. Listen to that still small voice speaking to you today. When you feel a tug on your heart and it won't go away, God is trying to get your attention.

2. Be courageous and defeat the fear that tries to steal your greater future. When change and chance are involved, fear will try to sneak in the back door. That's okay; your obedience will kick fear right out of the house.

3. Push yourself beyond your current levels of comfort. A greater you is just on the other side of comfortable!

4. When God calls, answer with expectancy! His plans for you are bigger than you could ever imagine on your own.

5. Be willing to let go of good and take hold of great! This is not easy, as good is comfortable. It requires an element of risk to let go in order to pursue great.

Today I encourage you to take these wonderful life lessons and run with them. I encourage you to step out of your comfort zone, see what God has in store for you and then trust, knowing His ways are greater than your ways.

GAME CHANGING MOVES:

1. What areas of your life are going well, but for some reason you feel you are just coasting? What can you do in these areas to move from good to great?

2. Moving from good to great doesn't take a drastic change in location, job or marital status. What can you do right now to get out of your comfort zone and really push yourself to a new level? This could be in your fitness, at your job, or in your sport.

3. Read and then write down the verses Jeremiah 29:11-13.

4. Read *Greater* by Steven Furtick.

GET UNCOMFORTABLE

I love to be comfortable. Rocking my sweats, tee shirt and tennis shoes is a way of life for this guy. Okay, I'm a PE teacher so that is appropriate attire. I also enjoy sleeping in a cold room with the ceiling fan on, while covered in cozy blankets. Yep, I just sent you to dreamland with that statement. I mean really, who doesn't like to be comfortable?

Now let me address a different kind of comfort. A kind of comfort that you enjoy (or endure) but can stifle who you are truly meant to be in life. What I'm talking about is getting to a level of comfort that says "I have arrived. I've made it, so I'll just chill out right where I'm at." Think about your own life or the lives of most people you know. For the majority of people, it looks like this; wake-up, go to work, come home, watch television and get in bed. Mix in eating and a couple sporting events for the kiddos, and that's life in a nutshell.

Don't get me wrong; there is nothing wrong with the life I've described above. My own life is similar in many ways, but for me, that kind of comfortable is not okay. I believe in being content but never comfortable to the point of "I have arrived or this is all there is to life." When you get to that point, you stop growing. When you stop growing you aren't able to develop all the incredible potential that lies dormant inside of you.

Here is how I equate this in my mind since I'm a "workout guy." When you perform strength training, it is tough, uncomfortable and takes effort. The training tears down your muscle fibers, and there is discomfort involved, but the result of that discomfort is new strength. You see, when your muscles fibers are torn down they must be repaired. As your body repairs the muscle fibers, they actually grow stronger. When your muscles grow stronger, you are then able to perform greater feats of strength than before.

This is the same thing that happens in life when you step out of your comfort zone. Getting outside of your comfort zone is tough; it takes effort, and it may tear you down a little, but the result is newfound strength. When you force yourself to get uncomfortable, you build the ability to perform greater feats than before. A good friend and mentor of mine put it this way in a recent conversation. *"Magic happens on the other side of comfort."* -Corby Stickelman

Shawnee Heights Wrestler Tristan Weaver and Coach Chad Parks. (2015)

Today I want to encourage you to get uncomfortable. I know that doesn't sound fun, but neither does living in a virtual groundhog day for the rest of your life. I believe God has placed unique gifts and talents inside of you that aren't being used or you've yet to discover, so make a decision to get uncomfortable and pursue a greater purpose in your life. Decide that today is the day you will break out of the chains of comfort that have been holding you captive for so long. Then dive headlong into the awesome future God has planned for you! It's not easy to purposely get uncomfortable, but it is worth it!

GAME CHANGING MOVES:

1. How often do you push yourself to get uncomfortable?

2. Do you feel you are using all the potential God has stored inside of you?

3. What can you do this week to get uncomfortable in order to make yourself stronger in the long run?

4. Read Matthew 19:20-23. Notice the young man was not willing to get uncomfortable in order to gain even more day the road. Would you have the same response?

PAIN WEEK

Each sport has a starting point and ending point to its season. Even if an athlete trains year-round, there is an actual competition season for their particular sport. As a wrestling coach, I can always feel the excitement building in my bones when the wrestling season start date arrives.

I'm sure many of my wrestlers have the same emotion building, but some also have a sense of trepidation for week one. My wrestlers have nicknamed the first week of practice "pain week." They gave the alpha week this dreadful name due to the fact that it is extremely difficult both mentally and physically. The application of the name is fitting in a way, yet it is not exactly true. Let me explain. Every physical activity and sport has its own unique level of difficulty and adjustment period. For example, football shape and wrestling shape are vastly different. Wrestling shape and track shape have a large variance as well. Each activity possesses its own specific movements and set of skills which often surprise the body, causing physical soreness and mental fatigue initially. However, after an adjustment period, the body learns the movements and skills, making the activity seem less difficult.

During the first week of wrestling, the athlete's bodies and minds begin the adjustment period. In the midst of this timeframe, the wrestlers will be tired, sore and fatigued both physically and mentally. In saying that, I'll also be very frank, wrestling is just downright tough. Almost everything about wrestling is difficult in some form or fashion. I mean drilling, live wrestling, conditioning and even moving mats are all vigorous activities. But I digress.

Now back to this whole "pain week" thing. Do I really run one? Although it may feel that way to some of the wrestlers, it is not the intent and that thought process is based on perception. Perception is based on perspective; therefore, perspective is an important factor to address with my wrestlers right away. Many wrestlers come in with a perspective that says "If I keep my head down and grind away, I'll make it through "pain week." This will indeed get most of them through that first week but not with the desired benefits or mental attitude. On the flipside, the perspective I desire for the wrestlers can be summed up and taught in these five bullet points:

1. Love for the sport- When a wrestler has love for the sport, then they are willing to go above and beyond to be the best. They embrace every aspect of wrestling and make a mental decision to enjoy it all.

2. Work Ethic- Work ethic is a skill needed in both wrestling and life. When a wrestler sees the value in great work ethic, they no longer look at hard work as punishment but rather improvement. When a wrestler has internal drive, they will push themselves to their limit every practice.

3. All In- An individual that has an all-in mentality is one who will do whatever it takes to reach his personal best. When a person is all-in, they won't give up or quit when it gets tough. Toe dippers, on the other hand, will jump ship as soon as the waters get rough.

4. Team Unity- Wrestling is unique in that it is an individual sport and team sport at the same time. The wrestlers who love their team will battle for their team. The team will drive them and bring out heart when it is needed most, and it will be needed. The difficulty level of wrestling, along with the literal blood, sweat and tears builds great team unity. Wrestlers who embrace team unity raise the level of everyone around them in both practice and competition.

5. Pride- Wrestlers who have personal pride realize that every action they take matters. They also do the right thing, not because they are forced to, but because they want to. Pride means doing all the little things right and understanding they add up to big things in the end.

When a wrestler adopts the five perspectives listed above, then "pain week" is no longer perceived as torture. It is still tough, but the perception changes from a "let me get through this" mindset to a "I'm going to embrace this" mindset.

Learning to embrace the grind and approaching the first week of a sport is applicable to every area of life. In life there will be seasons, some more difficult than others, but when a person decides to adopt the proper perspective, then they will embrace the grind and realize that where they are right now can be used to help them grow as human beings. Love, work ethic, being all-in, unity and pride are all mental attitudes that allow a person to succeed and grow in sports, business, parenting and more.

Today I encourage you to approach each season of your life with a great perspective and realize personal growth and success can seem painful, but ultimately they serve a great purpose in your life journey.

GAME CHANGING MOVES:

1. Take a look at your life and contemplate various seasons you've been through. These seasons can include good times, tough times and the in between.

2. Write down one or two takeaways you learned from those seasons.

3. Pick two of the five ideas in this chapter and work to apply them at a deeper level in your life this week, especially if they are fitting for the season you are currently in.

4. Read Romans 8:28 and Proverbs 14:23. How has God used all things for your good this year? What does Proverbs 14:23 teach you about hard work?

REPRESENT

During the summer, I get to work with a number of high school and college athletes. Many of these athletes work out with me for their off-season strength and conditioning. There are also a few who attend only my summer wrestling workouts.

While observing these athletes during training, I keep having a particular thought come into my mind. The thought goes something like this "You are representing 'something', but are you doing all you can to represent it well and to be the best example for others." This thought also takes me back to the mindset I possessed as a college athlete and still possess today.

When I was wrestling in college at Labette Community College and then Fort Hays State University, I knew what I was doing was about more than just me. As a college athlete, I was representing my God, my family, my school and my hometown. I always kept this in mind during training, competition, class and outside activities.

I remember being back home over Christmas break and working out with my dad's wrestling team. I would go to the school and get in my strength and conditioning workouts on my own, but when it came time for wrestling practice, I was in the room with athletes from my alma mater. This means I would do everything the coach (my dad) asked and do it with full intensity. Just like with my college wrestling team, I wanted to be the hardest worker in the room. I wanted to show the young bucks what it takes to be a champion and to work toward the fulfillment of their dreams. You see, I had the goal of becoming the first college All-American wrestler ever from my high school. I wanted to show the following generations exactly what is possible and how to get there. I mean, someone had to do it first. Someone had to lead the way and be the example of success on a higher level. This means my goal was bigger than me; it was about setting an example for others.

Now let's connect this same thought process to everyday life. Who are you representing? Do you feel like you are doing it well? What kind of example are you currently setting for others?

You are representing 'something', like it or not. You are representing your God, your family, the company you work for, your city, etc. The way you are representing these areas of life is setting an example for others around you. Someone or maybe many someones are watching you, and they will model what you do.

Shawnee Heights High School Wrestling Class 5A State Runner-Up team. Back from left to right: Coach Chad Parks, Coach Frank Crosson, Donnie Lockhart, Nick Meck, Dalton Mulligan, Isabel Holden, Harley Michael, Kayra Bernard, Marshal Hall, Brandon Flanagan, Coach Jeff Albers, Derek Holly, and Coach James Laster. Front from left to right: Cody Fritz, Derek Hammond Jr., Shane Herl, Justin Dyer, Aspen Kmiec, Tyler Willis, Austin Richards, and Bri Lockhart.

Don't get me wrong; none of us is perfect, and we will falter from time to time. That is no excuse to not try and be the best example we can be for others. We must be cognizant of who we represent and work our rear ends off to show others what is possible and what it takes to fulfill dreams.

Okay, back to my college days. I became the first college All-American wrestler from Pawhuska High School. Not only that, but I was a three-time Academic All-American and won over 100 college matches during my career as well.

So, guess what happened after I finished wrestling in college? Two more young men from my home town have gone on to become collegiate All-American wrestlers and academic All-Americans too. I cannot take credit for their awesome achievements, but I do hope my example lit a fire of possibility within their hearts and minds. Who you represent and the example you set will either embellish or diminish what others in your circle of influence see as possible. One of the greatest boxers and athletes of all time put it this way. *"Impossible is just a big word thrown around by small men who find it easier to live in the world they've been given than to explore the power they have to change it. Impossible is not a fact. It's an opinion. Impossible is not a declaration. It's a dare. Impossible is potential. Impossible is temporary. Impossible is nothing."* Muhammad Ali

Today, I challenge you to think about who you represent, how you represent and what example you are setting. Then work diligently to improve in all areas and show others what is truly possible in this life.

GAME CHANGING MOVES:

1. Write down a list of the people and places you represent.

2. Do you believe your actions are inspiring others to become more than they would be on their own?

3. Read and write down Colossians 3:23. Now determine to live a Colossians 3:23 life!

NO EXCUSES, NO EXPLANATIONS

Super Bowl winning coach Tony Dungy is one of my favorite coaches of all time. His calm demeanor and quiet strength are traits I admire and work to develop in myself as a coach, teacher, husband and parent.

Coach Dungy is also exceptionally quotable, and his quotes often relate to both sports and life in general. One of his quotes in particular has stuck with me since I first read it and keeps resurfacing in my mind. When that happens, I try to take heed and listen to what God is telling me personally or asking me to share in order to help someone else.

Here is the quote that keeps swimming laps around my brain. *"No Excuses. No Explanations."*

This quote is simple at first glance, yet its meaning can significantly impact your life. Below are two specific applications for the "No Excuses. No Explanations" quote that can impact in your life in a positive manner today.

1. **"No Excuses. No Explanations."**- Every individual needs to

take full responsibility for himself in all areas of life. Good or bad, own your decisions and leave out the excuses. If you mess up, then be willing to step up to the plate and admit you messed up. If you need to apologize for the mess up, then simply say "My bad, my fault, and I'm sorry." No excuses, no explanations; just own up and apologize.

2. "No Excuses. No Explanations."- There are times you will need to make tough decisions in life that you feel are best for you, your family or your team. These decisions may not be easy to make, they might not garner every one's support, and they might even bring ridicule your way. As long as you feel it is the correct decision, then don't fret and be sure you stick to your guns. You don't need to make excuses to appease others or try to explain yourself in order to win their approval.

I have worked on applying this no excuses, no explanations mentality into my life for the last couple of years. For example, if my wrestling team loses a meet and I personally know we have three varsity wrestlers sitting in the bench because of injury, I won't use that as an excuse. I could easily explain the situation to someone and they would understand how it influenced the team losing a meet, but there is no reason for me to explain and make excuses, so I just suck it up and take responsibility for the team loss. I mean really, I should have prepared them better, so it is my fault.

This is not easy as human nature wants to make excuses, point the finger, or explain in detail so people understand. But, not everything worth doing is going to be easy. I can tell you with full certainty that developing this mentality in your own life will ultimately bring about more mental freedom. It will also allow you to be open, honest and forthright with everyone around you. I think it might even be what some people would call growing up.

GAME CHANGING MOVES:

1. Write down two or three specific situations in your life where you often make excuses or feel you must explain yourself to others.

2. Over the next couple of days, journal before bed and write down anytime you made an excuse or over explained yourself.

3. Make a decision today to live a no excuses, no explanation lifestyle.

4. Read Mark 15 and see how Jesus is the ultimate example of no excuses, no explanations.

NO LIMITATION
AS LIMITATION

"Using no way as way, having
no limitation as limitation."
Bruce Lee

This is such a simple yet profound quote by legendary martial artist Bruce Lee. Although the entire quote is fantastic, I only want to address the second half which states "Having no limitation as limitation."

In theory, Bruce Lee was saying we need to stop using our perceived limitations as excuses. How many of us, including me, have used a supposed limitation as an excuse for failure or maybe to never begin something in the first place?

In sports, the limitations and excuses may sound something like this, "I'm too slow, I'm not tall enough or he is stronger than me." In everyday life, the limitations and excuses my sound like this, "I don't have enough time, I don't have enough money or I don't have the right connections."

Each restrictive weakness listed above can be looked at as a real limitation or valid excuse, but according to Bruce Lee, that doesn't get you off the hook. He wants you to know that what you perceive as a limitation cannot be used to bind or restrict you. You must find a way to succeed, despite the so-called limitation. You have to stop making excuses and find a way to get it done.

This brings to mind wisdom from successful businessman and author Ron Reynolds when he penned the words "People will find a way to do exactly what they need to do." You see, when you really need to get something done, you'll find a way.

Both Bruce Lee and Ron Reynolds know people have a plethora of self-imposed limitations. Many have trouble succeeding or making necessary changes in life because they use these limitations as excuses, but ultimately people have the ability to choose and overcome the limitation in order to find success.

Today I encourage you to take the limitations off your mind, rid yourself of excuses and find a way. Declare that you will no longer use your "limitations" as limiting factors in your life!

GAME CHANGING MOVES:

1. Write down 2-3 limitations you might have as an athlete, coach, parent, businessman, etc.

2. Write down ways to work around these limitations or actually use them to help you succeed in life.

3. Read Exodus 4:10-17. How does God keep Moses from using a supposed limitation as a limitation?

VISION

"Where there is no vision the people will perish."
Proverbs 29:18

That scripture was written on a poster-board sign that hung on the wall of the Pawhuska Middle School wrestling room. It had been hanging there as far back as I can remember. My dad was the coach, so I was in that wrestling room on a daily basis for most of my childhood.

Every time I entered the wrestling room I'd purposely go over and look at that sign, and there were many instances where the sign would catch my attention during practice as well. Each time I would read the words and wonder what they might mean and why they were in the wrestling room. In my young mind, I assumed the words meant if you lose your eyesight, then you'll die. Morbid, right?

So why is that hanging in the wrestling room, and what was my dad thinking?

When I moved into high school and we were in a different wrestling room. I didn't see that sign anymore, but for some reason, the words never escaped my memory. It's not that I thought about them often, but they were still there in the recesses of my mind. From time to time I'd see that sign in my mind and think about the words written upon it.

It wasn't until I was in college that I ran into those words again, while reading through a study on the book of Proverbs. That's when it clicked! That's when I understood what Proverbs 29:18 meant and also why my dad had the sign hanging in the middle school wrestling room. The words had nothing to do with eyesight, but more to do with foresight.

I was a college wrestler at the time and wanted to become an All-American; that was my pursuit, my dream, and my vision. Ah ha.... my vision! My vision was big, would take a ton of work and dedication, and was maybe even outside the realm of my own talents. This vision was big enough to scare me and let me know I needed God to help me out; it also made me feel alive!

So, what did that have to do with Proverbs 29:18? Everything! Proverbs 29:18 states, *"Where there is no vision the people will perish."*

You see, I believe God wants you to have a vision. He wants you to dream and have a vision that drives you. When you have a vision, then you are really living. When you don't have a vision that drives you, you are not living, you're merely existing. When you merely exist, then you are just waiting around until you perish.

This same thought process was also stated in the words of the great warrior of Scotland William Wallace, "All men die, but not all men really live."

Today I encourage you to dream big and strive to fulfill the vision God has placed in your mind and upon your heart. I challenge you to develop a vision and dream so grand it scares you. This should be a vision you want to work your hardest to fulfill, but you also know that apart from the Lord's help, it's just not going to happen.

I did fulfill my vision of becoming an All-American wrestler, but life didn't begin or end with the completion of that vision. God just placed new visions in my mind and upon my heart. These visions are big enough to scare me and also make me realize I need His help in order to fulfill them in this lifetime, but I'll gladly dedicate myself to the work of fulfilling these visions and truly live.

This chapter is about my vision, but I hope it serves as a sign that catches your attention and makes you wonder. What do these words mean and why are they important in my life? Why is this sign in front of me at this very moment, and what can I do about it?

GAME CHANGING MOVES:

1. Do you have a vision for your life? What is it? Write down the vision you have and place it where you'll see it daily, like a bathroom mirror.

2. Ask yourself "Am I truly living or merely existing?"

3. Read Proverbs 29:18 and Habakkuk 2:3. How do these scriptures relate to your vision? Does Habakkuk 2:3 guarantee the vision will be fulfilled on your personal time table?

LOVE IN ACTION

After my freshman year of college, I decided to transfer from Missouri Valley College to a new school. I liked Missouri Valley but decided to attend a school closer to home. I was a college wrestler, so I transferred to Labette Community College, which had long been a powerhouse in wrestling and was only two hours from my hometown.

When I arrived at Labette I was filled with excitement and a hunger to get going, but upon arrival there was one major snafu; I didn't have place to stay. Yep, there had been a mess up in paperwork, and immediately I was a homeless college student. Thankfully my new wrestling coach pulled some strings and found a room I could rent with a family in town. They were awesome for renting out a space, and I was grateful to have a roof over my head, but I still had a real issue to deal with in my boarding adventure. How was I going to pay for this room?

Fast forward to Christmas break. I was back home with my family in Oklahoma when my dad received an unexpected phone call. On the other end of the line was a man named Earl Brunger who we attended church with each week. He asked my dad if we'd like to come over and have lunch with his family that day. My dad accepted, and off we went to get some grub and good fellowship. When we arrived, my dad was surprised with a blast from his past. At our friend's house was a man named Roger Swearengin. My dad had been friends with Roger until the 8th grade, but then Roger moved away and that was that.

Now some 30 years later, the two long-lost friends stood face to face. They began to catch up and reignited their friendship in no time at all. Cool, right? Well, here is where the story gets even better. Roger told my dad he lived in the same town where I was currently attending college. He had seen my name in the local paper for wrestling at the college and wondered if we might be related, so Roger contacted his relative, Earl, in his old hometown and the connection was confirmed.

Moments after I met Roger that day, he offered (more like insisted) to have me stay with his family for the rest of my time at school. My dad asked what I thought, and I let him and Roger know I was truly obliged. Then I asked Roger what the charge was going to be for renting a room in his home. He started to laugh and said "Charge? What charge? Son, you are welcome to live under my roof and eat home cooked meals each night, free of charge."

Wait, what? Free of charge. Was this dude crazy or something? Well if Roger was crazy, then I was willing to risk it for the room and board cost of nothing down and nothing owed. Later that week I headed back to school and moved into my new digs. When I arrived at the residence I got to meet the rest of the family, which included Roger's wife Cathy and his daughter Leigh. I'm going to pause here for a second in this story, because of Leigh. She was an 18-year-old senior in high school and I was a 19-year-old second year college student. Oh yeah, she just happened to be beautiful too. So maybe Roger and Cathy were crazy. Thankfully they were not crazy, just very trusting people. The entire family treated me like one of their own from the get go. They supplied my room, home-cooked meals, friendship, guidance and heartfelt love. These three made me part of their family.

So, what is the point of this chapter beyond it being a good story? Here is the point. When was the last time you did something for someone who couldn't repay you?

You see, when I was a poor college student struggling to eat, there were people who stepped up and helped out. These people went out of their way, got uncomfortable, and jumped into action. They didn't have to do so and really, they were taking a risk. I mean they were now spending extra money on food, water, electricity, etc. They brought in a 19-year-old young man they really didn't know and allowed him to live under the same roof with their sweetheart of an 18-year-old daughter. That alone might have made me say no way as a dad. Yet they took me in with open arms and did it with nothing but grace and love.

This family truly showed me heartfelt love and did it expecting nothing in return. Bottom line, what they really did was speak volumes about Christ's love in both word and action. You see, Roger, Cathy and Leigh believed in Jesus, they believed in the words written in Scripture and they lived it out loud. That's why Roger wasn't worried about this young guy coming into his home; he knew I was a believer too. He knew he could do more than just help me financially; he could also be an example of Jesus to me. Well, he sure got the job done.

My heart is truly overwhelmed and grateful as I pen the words in this book. There is nothing I can ever do to repay this family for their love and generosity, but I can follow their example, which is to walk Christ's love toward others. In doing so, I have the opportunity to pay it forward and help someone who cannot help me in return. Today I encourage you to learn from and live out the example laid out in this story. Make up your mind to reach out and help someone knowing that you will get nothing in return. In this way, you too will be an example of Christ's love and make this a better world to live in for all.

"A new command I give you: Love one another. As I have loved you, so you must love one another. By this everyone will know that you are my disciples, if you love one another." -John 13: 34-35

"Do not forget to show hospitality to strangers, for by so doing some people have shown hospitality to angels without knowing it." -Hebrews 13:2

Thank you Roger, Cathy, and Leigh Swearengin Harvey for your hospitality, friendship and love. You are an amazing family and live out your faith in word and deed daily. I love you.

GAME CHANGING MOVES:

1. When is the last time you've done something for someone who cannot repay you?

2. What can you do today to show an act of truly selfless love?

3. Read the Parable of the Good Samaritan in Luke 10:25-37

4. What does love in action look like to you? Write it out and then act on it at least one day this week.

FIVE SMOOTH STONES

Some memories are so thick they almost seem tangible. Yet, like all memories, even the tangible ones are shrouded in fog. One such memory takes a journey through my mind from time to time and the impact of that moment is as real today as when the event took place. In all actuality, the impact is greater today than it was at the time of conception. Time and wisdom have made it so.

The year was 1995, and I was a junior in high school. It was December, and I had just returned home from wrestling practice; tired and hungry as was the norm for that time of year. Across the street our neighbors pulled into their drive as I was walking into the house. I paused for a moment to wave and say hello as these people were more than just neighbors; they were mentors and what I would consider family. They waved back and replied with a quick greeting. As I turned to walk into the house, I heard a voice say "Chad, when you have a moment, please come over and visit with me." The voice was that of the aforementioned neighbor, Mrs. LaVerne Core.

When Mrs. Core asked me to do something, anything, there was no hesitation on my part. Mrs. Core was like a grandmother to me and a woman I loved dearly. I tremendously respected her and appreciated any opportunity to visit. So, I hustled in the house, told my parents I was running over to the Core's and then bolted across the street. Yes, Mrs. Core was more important than dinner for a teenage wrestler who didn't have to weigh in for a couple of days. That's serious business right there!

Upon my arrival, Mrs. Core motioned me in the house, and I took a seat in the same spot I had sat in every time I'd visited that house since I was in the 6th grade. This was my spot; it was adjacent to Mrs. Core's chair and Mr. Core's chair beside hers. Words cannot do justice to the feeling that would overcome me when I sat in that chair time and again, but for now, I will assign the word 'peace' to the emotion. I still feel that way when I visit the Core's house.

Mrs. Core looked at me for a moment, reached over and grabbed a small gray bag off her side table, then looked back at me again. After a brief pause, she spoke and the following dialogue ensued... "Chad, I've been thinking about you. Do you know the story of David and Goliath in the Bible?"

"Yes Ma'am."

"Chad, you are David in that story. You are young, courageous and able to slay any giant with God's help."

I have to admit, at that moment, I didn't know what to say or really what Mrs. Core meant by those words. Then she looked down at the gray bag in her delicate hands and said, "This bag is full of small smooth stones. I imagine these stones are just like the ones David used to kill Goliath. I want you to have this bag and its contents." "Thank you, Mrs. Core," was all I could say while my mind was trying to comprehend the significance of the gift.

"Chad, here is what I want you to do. Any time you are in a situation and need God's strength, think about these stones. Ask God to help you as He helped David. If you are in the middle of a wrestling match or anywhere else in life and need God to help you, just ask and He'll be there."

At that very moment, I fully understood the significance of the gray bag filled with stones. Mrs. Core's words, coupled with the material object, drove the point home in my teenage heart, but what I failed to understand at the time was the second lesson Mrs. Core was teaching me. Through her example, Mrs. Core was showing me how to build into the life of another person. She was instilling in me firsthand the importance of taking the time to pour into the hearts and minds of others.

That, my friends, is the reason I stated in the opening of this chapter that this vivid memory has a greater impact on me today than it did when the actual event transpired. It wasn't until I was an adult that I looked back and fully understood all Mrs. Core had intentionally taught me that day.

So today, I want to encourage you in two areas. The first is to take the advice of Mrs. Core, taught through the story of David and Goliath. Know you can call on God at any time, and He will be there to hear and respond on your behalf. The second is to intentionally take the time to pour into someone else's life. They might not fully understand what you are doing for them right now, but in time it will be revealed in their hearts and minds.

"Then David took his shepherd's staff, selected five smooth stones from the brook, and put them in the pocket of his shepherd's pack, and with his sling in his hand approached Goliath." -1 Samuel 17:40

GAME CHANGING MOVES:

1. Who is building or has built into your life in a positive and impactful way?

2. Call or write that person today and let them know how much you appreciate all they have done for you.

3. Read the story of David and Goliath in 1 Samuel 17. What is your favorite part of the story?

SUPERHEROES

I have a lifelong infatuation with superheroes. I'm not exactly sure when this affinity began, but I can tell you it's been running strong as far back as my memory allows.

When I was a young man, we used to visit my Grandpa Morgan's house in Tecumseh, Ok. He lived out in the country on a few acres and raised horses for a living. Visiting Grandpa Morgan's was fun, and I have some good memories from those trips. One of the strongest recollections in my mind is laying on the floor with all my cousins watching old Superman movies until late in the evening. My grandpa had a large collection of these Superman flicks, and we always took advantage of watching them while at his house. I believe this was possibly the birthplace for my devotion to Superman, my favorite male superhero.

Superman is big, strong and he can flat out kick some rear end. He is the kind of man all men want to become one day. He is like a dad, coach, teacher and mentor all wrapped into one. Superman has it going on!

That said, what about women; is there a female superhero women look up to and want to become one day? Is it Superwoman, Wonder Woman, Aurora, or some other superheroine that makes a young girl say "One day I'll be like her!"?

I am not female, so I can in no way answer that question. What I can tell you is this- there are many superheroines out there in the world who actually exist outside of the movies and comic books. These ladies are like a mother, coach, teacher and mentor all wrapped into one, and sometimes they really are each of those. These real-life superheroines might not wear spandex and capes, but under their street clothes is a woman who is shaping the world and making it a better place.

I am very fortunate to have been raised by a superheroine as well as being married to one. My mother, LaCrecia Parks, was the first female superhero in my life and through her I experienced the strength God has placed into women. My mom is a mighty woman with a heart so big it barely fits in her body. God also blessed me with a powerhouse wife who pulls off superhero feats on a daily basis. She constantly amazes me with her ability to make being a wife, mother and leader so effortless. Both of these women exhibit superhero traits such as bravery, courage, selflessness, and servant leadership in their lives. They are the ultimate exhibition of individual strength and teamwork all wrapped up into one awesome heroine ready to take on the world and then give the kids a bath later that night.

Women are simply amazing. God has placed within them the capacity to love deeply, empathize with others, correct when needed, create life and much more. A woman can work all day, take care of her children, prepare dinner, clean the house, pay the bills, save a family from a burning building and stop a bank robbery. Okay, maybe a couple of those are from superhero movies, but I have no doubt a woman could complete the tasks if called upon to get it done.

If we look at the Bible, we'll see multiple examples of women who pulled off superhero feats, influencing their society and the world. Mary, the mother of Jesus, is the perfect example of the female superhero elite. She had a baby, raised him to a man, watched him sacrifice his life on the cross and then helped his disciples carry on the mission God commissioned them to complete. She was a woman who lived a selfless life and also showed servant leadership through her deeds. Mary allowed herself to be used by God to make the greatest contribution to mankind the world has ever known. Even though Mary lived 2000 years ago, her impact is still felt today and will be through eternity.

Another Biblical superheroine is found in the old testament book of Esther. In this story, Queen Esther bravely risked her own life by going before the King and asking for help to save her cousin from death. The request was much larger than just saving her cousin; it actually stopped a bad man (Haman) from destroying the Jewish people. Esther's faith and courage was an act of heroism that saved her people from what would have been certain death under normal circumstances. Thankfully, Esther was no normal person; she was a superheroine in action.

Beyond the Bible, the world is full of female superheroes who have helped shape life as we know it today. Some of these ladies are famous and others have led lives of obscurity, yet each has impacted the humanity greatly. Whether Oprah, Mother Teresa, or your next-door neighbor, female superheroes exist and are working tirelessly to make this world a better place for both you and me. I have two daughters of my own, and I want them to know that they are incredible in many ways. I want these young ladies to understand God has created them with a special beauty that goes beyond outside appearance. They, along with all women, have been created with an immeasurable amount of courage, bravery, strength, selflessness, intelligence and the ability to lead others with empathy and love. I want my beautiful daughters to realize the sky's the limit for their lives and God has a great purpose for them in this world. It is my deepest desire for my daughters to recognize God has given them superhero abilities, and these abilities can help make this world a better place for all.

She is clothed with strength and dignity; she can laugh at the days to come. She speaks with wisdom, and faithful instruction is on her

Ally (age 7) and Kate (age 9) Super Heroines

tongue. She watches over the affairs of her household and does not eat the bread of idleness. Her children arise and call her blessed; her husband also, and he praises her: 'Many women do noble things, but you surpass them all." - Proverbs 31:25-29

Below is a writing I completed a few years ago for Mya Thompson, daughter of my friend Joel Thompson and for my daughters Kate and Ally. This freestyle poem is also dedicated to all the superheroines out there changing the world!

✷ *The Girl Who Can Will...*

You young lady are a shining star. When you walk into a room, it is filled with light. Your mere presence is like the dawning of day as it ends the night.

God has given you personality and heart the size of Texas. You possess a true compassion to help others, while seeking nothing in return. This is a valuable gift from God that will allow you to make a positive impact upon all those you meet in this life.

You love to read, sing, and compete in sports. You're smart as a whip and tough as nails, both traits handed down from your mother and father. Superior genetics passed on to their daughter!

Your goals are vast, and you have dreams a plenty. The zest you possess for life is contagious for all who have the privilege of crossing your path. These unique characteristics make you beautifully you, one of God's greatest creations under His skies so blue.

I want you to know you can be anything in this life you desire to be. You can be a pediatrician who heals, a teacher who helps or maybe an author who writes her own books. Your mind is the limit so let it run free; you can be anything in this life you desire to be.

You young lady are the girl who can. No I take that back, you young lady are the girl who will!

GAME CHANGING MOVES:

1. What characteristics do you think would make the ultimate female superhero?

2. Write down a list of women who have been a positive influence in your life. Which of these women is the ultimate superhero to you?

3. Make a commitment to either call or write a letter to 2-3 of the most influential women in your life and thank them for how they have helped develop you as a person.

4. Read Proverbs 31:10-31. What stands out the most to you in these verses?

BE THE LIGHT

You know the type, right? The person who is undoubtedly refreshing and a joy to be around. Their presence lights up the room with an invisible yet inexplicably evident glow that creates warmth in your soul. This is the person you love to see and always walk away from feeling better than when you arrived. I can only explain them as a light that cannot be hidden.

I believe each person can become what I've described above. Some people might have the "it" factor, of this I'm not certain, but I am confident in stating that if each person worked to be the light in the community, this world would be a brighter place to live. In that vein, I believe there are some simple steps that can be taken to become a light.

Five practical ways to become a light in your community:

1. Smile- In the words of Mother Teresa "Every time you smile at someone, it is an action of love, a gift to that person, a beautiful thing." Science also agrees with the dear Saint. Neurological science tells us we have in our brain's mirror neurons. These neurons cause us to mirror what we see with our face and bodies. This can explain the way people are looking at you. If you are smiling, they will most likely smile too. If you're walking around mean mugging, then that's what you'll get in return. I have to admit this is a constant battle for me, as I often look serious and stoic. The good news is, it's easy and fun to work on making yourself smile more often.

2. Speech- "Let your conversation be gracious and attractive so that you will have the right response for everyone." - Colossians 4:6. What you say and how you say it speaks volumes to those around you. Words can bless, and words can curse. We must always be cognizant of the words we use, as they all have power in some form or fashion. When you learn to speak with graciousness toward people, then you have a much greater chance of impacting them in a positive manner. Using your words to build people up will allow the light to shine.

3. Genuinely care about people- I know, crazy, right? When you care about people, it is evident and can be felt. Philippians 2:4 says "Do not merely look out for your own personal interests, but also for the interests of others." When you really care about others, then their best interests becomes important to you too.

4. Decide to be happy- Yes, happiness is a decision. It is a vastly important decision that influences your emotions, which in turn guides your actions. I will not attempt to explain this any better than did Martha Washington when she stated "I am determined to be cheerful and happy in whatever situation I may find myself. For I have learned that the greater part of our misery or unhappiness is determined not by our circumstance but by our disposition." When you decide to be happy, your light shines brightly for all to see.

5. Get it out there ASAP- Get what out there? Well, have you ever been sitting and all the sudden you think something good about someone? Did you let them know what you were thinking? Determine right now that you'll never keep those good thoughts to yourself and cheat your friend of a blessing. Instead, let the person know your good thoughts about them right away in person, via phone call or text. When you are generous with your praise and appreciation, everyone around you is better for it.

I cannot think of a better way to end this chapter than to once again quote Mother Teresa, a shining example of this message. "Spread love everywhere you go. Let no one ever come to you without leaving happier." In so doing you'll become a light that cannot be hidden, providing both refreshing and warmth for the soul.

GAME CHANGING MOVES:

1. Who is the kindest and most loving person you know? What characteristics give them this distinction in your mind? Write down those characteristics.

2. Look at the five-point list in this chapter and pick out two areas you need to work on starting now. Focus on these areas all week long and see if they become habitual for you.

3. Read Colossians 4:6. What does this wisdom mean for you in today's world culture?

YOU CAN
CHOOSE
YOUR MOOD

I'm in the middle of coaching at a wrestling tournament, and one of my wrestlers loses a close match. Soon afterward I'm walking down a narrow aisle when I run into a coaching friend of mine, Coach Charles Knox.

Coach Knox says "Hey Coach, good to see you," and gives me a handshake and hug like he always does when we cross paths. Upon backing away, he says "Everything okay? You look mad." I told Coach Knox that one of my wrestlers had just lost a tough match, and he said "I understand, I've been there."

We parted ways, but his words "you look mad" stuck in my head and wouldn't leave.

Suddenly the thought hit me. I'm not going to walk around mad, instead I'm going to choose to be happy right now! I can't tell you

I'll ever be "happy" when one of my wrestlers loses a match, but what I can tell you is I have the ability to decide how long I let a negative emotion hold me hostage. Harboring a negative emotion is not beneficial for me or anyone else. Personally, it makes me feel bad both physically and mentally. Beyond that, others can sense the bad mood as well.

When I looked at this situation, I realized that if Coach Knox could sense my bad mood, then my wrestlers could sense it as well, and that's not fair to them. They need their coach to be on top of his game and ready to help them succeed.

Thankfully there is good news and a light of hope for a mere mortal like me. There is hope because I know if I can train my brain to hold a negative emotion, then I can also train it to capture a positive one as well. You see, brain research has proven the mind is pliable and malleable.

What does that mean? It simply means we can retrain our brain as it is not a fixed object. Mind you, retraining your brain starts with a personal choice.

But let's get back to Coach Knox. I'm walking down the same narrow aisle about 30 minutes after I first ran into Coach Knox and we had our brief conversation. This time he sees me and says "There it is; that smile is back. That's what I like to see, Coach Parks!"

Now my thoughts start running one hundred miles per hour about how this situation connects to life outside of wrestling.

We all have situations in life that bring us down, make us mad or evoke other negative emotions. When these situations occur, we have the power to make a choice. We can choose to stay in a negative state of mind and let it bring us and others down, or we can choose to let go of the negative emotion and be happy.

I know this is easier said than done and it might be a situation more serious than losing a wrestling match. The situation could be deal-

Tristan Weaver and Coach Parks laughing as Tristan gets some blood cleaned off his forehead. (2015)

ing with an injury, the loss of a job, working in a bad environment, etc., but the choice is still yours and you have to decide if you want to reside in a negative state of mind or maintain a good attitude. That's what it ultimately boils down to. Your decision, your choice.

My hope is that you will make a choice to let go of the anger, hurt, pain, fear or whatever negative emotion might be holding you hostage.

I hope you choose to be happy today and let the world say "There it is, that smile is back! That's what I like to see!"

GAME CHANGING MOVES:

1. Do you let your emotions control you, or do you control your emotions?

2. What situations are you in on a regular basis that cause you to lose your joy?

3. What choice can you make to change your reaction in those situations?

4. Read Proverbs 15:23 and Proverbs 17:22. What do these scriptures tell you about joy?

5. Read *The Happiness Advantage* by Shawn Archor.

WHAT YOU TAKE IN IS WHAT COMES OUT

"If we don't think right, we don't act right. When we don't act right, then we don't attract the right people into our lives." Mike Wade, former college football coach and Vice President of Sales at Advo-Care International.

Before I dig deeper, I want you to ponder the following questions from your own life:

- Who are the five people you hang around with the most?
- What kind of books do you read?
- What are you watching on television, YouTube, or social media?
- What music are you listening to on a regular basis?

You see, each of the areas mentioned above influences how you think. How you think influences your actions. Your actions determine the kind of person you are and therefore the kind of person you attract. What you put in is what will eventually come out.

Ancient wisdom tells us this is true.

"Above all else, guard your heart, for everything you do flows from it." Proverbs 4:23

Now let me personalize this thought process. When I looked at and answered these questions, I quickly discovered what is most beneficial for me to be at my best as a human being. What I uncovered is I like up people, up books, up music, and up television. When I say "up", I am referring to that which is uplifting and will build the inner man. When I fill my mind with up, then my attitude goes up as well. It's pretty simple really; put in good and good comes out.

On the flip side, there have been times in my life when I've allowed down people, books, music and television into my world. During those times, I wasn't intentional about what I was taking in and the kind of person I was becoming. So, as I let junk in, junk came out. My attitude and actions reflected who I was at that moment, not who I really wanted to be. For example, when I was a young man, I listened to a lot of music with explicit lyrics and messages filled with anger and sexual content. It just so happens that as I devoured this music, the anger inside me grew and so did the way I viewed females. Now, I will not blame my actions on the music as I made a choice to listen to it, but content of the music did form a mindset in me that was not healthy in many ways and where the mind goes, the body soon follows.

You know what is great about this information? You have a choice in the matter. You can choose the people you kick it with on a daily basis. You can choose the books you read, the music you listen to and the television you watch. Since you can choose and these choices influence the person you are and will become, then it makes sense to choose that which builds you up.

Today I encourage you to get honest with yourself about what you are letting into your heart each day. Be forthright about the person you are becoming and if it's who you want to be. Then get intentional about the people you spend time with, the books you read, the music you listen to and what you are watching. When you do this, your attitude and world can change for the better.

GAME CHANGING MOVES:

1. Review the four questions at the beginning of this chapter and answer them honestly.

2. In what ways can you improve in each area listed?

3. Read Proverbs 4:23. What does this Scripture mean?

4. Jump into action today because everything you do matters, and every second counts.

MAKE
LEMONADE

In the previous chapter I wrote about liking up music, up books, up people, etc. In this chapter, I want to focus in a little more on up people.

We all know people who are up people. These people are positive, uplifting and they just make you feel good. They are the kind of people who embody the saying "when life gives you lemons, make lemonade."

On the flip side, we all know people who are "vampires." These people suck the life and energy out of a room and make you feel bad. They are the kind of people who embody the saying "when life gives you lemonade, make lemons."

Today I want to encourage you to be an up person and not a vampire. I'm sorry if I have offended any real vampires by comparing you to people who are downers.

Life is full of ups and downs, highs and lows, peaks and valleys, etc. The good news is that it's not the deciding factor of the attitude you possess. You are the deciding factor. This means you can possess and exhibit a making lemonade attitude in good times and in bad; it's your choice.

I fully believe it takes deliberate practice to embody and display this positive attitude. I also believe it starts in your mind, and the genesis is what you feed your mind. Therefore, I want to encourage you to start feeding your mind good and not bad. Inventory what you are watching, reading, listening to and who you are around. If any of those areas are not where or what they should as far as adding true positive value to your life, then make a change.

Taking lemons and making lemonade may not come naturally to you, but that's no excuse not to work on it! You are the deciding factor and if nothing changes, nothing changes.

It's time to take your lemons and make lemonade!

GAME CHANGING MOVES:

1. Ask yourself this question and be 100% honest "am I am up person or an energy vampire?"

2. What changes can you make in your life to become an up person?

3. Read the Parable of the Sower in Matthew 13. Do you think Jesus was an up person? What makes you think He was or wasn't an up person?

4. Read *The Energy Bus* by Jon Gordon

THE WAY YOU DO ANYTHING IS THE WAY YOU DO EVERYTHING

Recently I was reading a few posts on social media and saw a statement from a leader I respect named Joe Hadachek, a football coach and businessman. His impactful words follow.

"The way you do anything is the way you do everything."

Following that statement was a picture of a messy rack of kettlebells and a picture of an organized rack of kettlebells.

"YES" was the immediate thought in my head after reading the statement and seeing the pictures. As a longtime coach and workout freak I have seen people take pride in their facilities and equipment, and I've also seen people take little to no pride in their facilities and equipment.

That said, the statement written by Coach Hadachek goes much deeper than the organization of kettlebells or the weight room. The deeper meaning here is that the way you complete any task, whether highly meaningful or seemingly menial, says a lot about who you are as a person. How you complete a task often correlates with how much you care about something. Ultimately, the way you complete a task has an impact on your level of success in life.

Let's look at this principle when applied to some real-life scenarios:

- Messy room, house or car equals disorganization in everything you do.
- Lazy, sloppy and partial effort in practice equals lazy, sloppy and partial effort in a game or match.
- Lazy, sloppy and partial effort at work equals lazy, sloppy and partial effort in your work performance.

This list could go on and on.

Now don't get me wrong, I'm not talking about perfectionism. Perfectionism is not the desired process or mandatory for success in life. Rather the desired process is to do your absolute best in all situations, thus leading to success.

Today I encourage you to keep in mind the simple yet profound wisdom of a highly successful leader... the way you do anything is the way you do everything!

GAME CHANGING MOVES:

1. Make your bed every morning upon waking. This task is under your control, and it's an easy habit to add into your daily routine. You've got to start somewhere.

2. Clean out your car in the next two days. Then work to keep it clean on a regular basis.

3. Clean out and organize your refrigerator. This will give you a much needed spark to get going in bigger areas of life.

4. Read Proverbs 14:23 and Colossians 3:23. Hard work applies to everything we do in life.

THE MOWING OLYMPICS

The Mowing Olympics. That's a real thing, right?

I vividly remember mowing yards in the scorching mid-summer Oklahoma heat. My dad and I cut grass and painted houses each summer during my youth; dad focused most of his time and energy on painting while I held down the yard work.

We mowed between 25-30 yards each week, all with a push mower. We didn't have the luxury of a riding mower back then. I would often push mow five or more yards in a day all by myself; this included mowing, trimming, edging and sweeping off the sidewalks with a broom. We didn't get a leaf blower until I was older.

The job was physically taxing, but I always enjoyed mowing yards and took pride in my work. While cutting grass I had two focus points in my mind, to finish the yard as quickly as possible and to make it beautiful.

As I looked to accomplish both focus points, I would often have a specific scenario running through my mind. The Mowing Olympics! I would imagine I was going to be a competitor in the Mowing

Olympics, and this was training for the contest. The Mowing Olympics gold medal would go to the mow-athlete who finished the yard in the least amount of time and made it look the best. That portion would be decided by judges. Yes, I'm serious. I really did this while mowing.

Maybe it was the Oklahoma heat index, maybe it was a coping mechanism or maybe it was something far more important taking place in my mind during my summer Olympic mowing experiences. I'd like to believe it was the latter.

What I was learning while cutting all those yards and preparing myself for the Mowing Olympics set the stage for the rest of my life as an athlete, coach, parent and businessman. Sounds nutty, right? Well, let me share with you five lessons I learned during these heated summer sessions:

1. Preparation takes place in the backyard. People often see success and assume it is because a person is talented or has received some special breaks. What they don't realize is that the person has put in hours and hours of work behind the scenes. This person been working and perfecting their craft in the backyard of life where the public eye can't see them. Then when opportunities arise, they pounce on them as a lion does his prey.

2. You are responsible for motivating you. It is great to have others inspire you to become better, but real motivation comes from within. You cannot wait for a cheerleader to help you get to work; that's just not real life. Cheerleaders are great and we all need them, but sometimes you have to work alone.

3. Take pride in your work. No matter what you are doing in life, it represents who you are as a person. If you give full focus and effort to any job, people see that and will be inspired. They will see you take pride in all you do, and hopefully they'll do the same.

4. You are always training. You may or may not realize it, but you are always training for something in life. You cannot always control what that something will be, but you can control how you train so train well!

5. Embrace the process. Mow, trim, edge, sweep and repeat. This process can get old week after week, but it is necessary to make a yard beautiful. In order to reach your full potential in life, you must learn to embrace the process of becoming great. It's not always sexy or fun, but it is necessary for success.

Okay, I know you are wracked with anticipation in wanting to know if I ever won the Mowing Olympics. Well I have good news for you; I did! I am a multi-time Olympic Mowing Champion. Now to be fair, I was the only person entered into the Mowing Olympic Games, but I still won. Really, that in itself is a wonderful lesson as we are often our own greatest competition.

GAME CHANGING MOVES:

1. What life experiences have helped form you into the person you are today? Write down at least two of them and think about what you have learned from each experience.

2. Read 1 Corinthians 9:27. How does this wisdom apply to the work you do on a daily basis?

3. Read *Chop Wood, Carry Water* by Joshua Medcalf.

TRUE GRIT

Grit.

Could this be the most important key to Success?

According to Dr. Angela Duckworth, Professor of Psychology at the University of Pennsylvania, grit might be the most important factor for success in life. Dr. Duckworth and a team of researchers intentionally traveled to some of the most challenging settings available in order to study both children and adults in search of predictors of success. The studies were conducted with two key thoughts in mind: who would be successful in these settings, and why?
The studies were conducted with cadets at West Point, contestants at the Scripps National Spelling bee, rookie teachers in tough neighborhoods and employees of private companies. Data was collected in numerous areas during the studies, and one characteristic stood out above the rest as a predictor of success.

The top characteristic leading to success in all studies wasn't social intelligence, good looks, physical health or IQ. It was plain old grit.

So, what exactly is grit?

Dr. Duckworth describes grit as passion and perseverance for very long term goals. She also states grit has the following attributes or markers:

- Stamina
- Sticking with your future day in and day out for years.
- Working really hard to make that future a reality.
- Living life like a marathon rather than a sprint.

As a long time athlete, coach and teacher, I believe in grit and understand it does lead to success. My dad always said "Standardized testing cannot measure a student's work ethic and intestinal fortitude, but those are the things that make a person succeed in school, sports, and life."

Basically, he was saying what Dr. Duckworth's studies have proven. Grit leads to success.

Coach Jeff Albers and Coach Chad Parks congratulate Shawnee Heights High School wrestler Jake Patterson on a big win. (2015)

There is one question left unanswered by Dr. Duckworth's study. How do we build grit? Dr. Duckworth says she's not sure, and therefore we must be gritty about studying grit. Good answer. Below are seven thoughts on building grit for yourself, your team and your family.

1. Paint Vision- This means building a dream, allowing others to dream and having a plan to reach that dream. When people can connect a dream to their passion, then they are more willing to persevere for a long period of time. Action steps also need to be attached when you are painting vision. You don't have to see every stair, but you need to know where the staircase is located.

2. Take Care Of Business- Do the little things right every single day because they will add up to something big.

3. Make a decision and stick to it- When you have a decided heart, you'll also have the grit needed to see you through on the journey.

4. Encourage others and yourself- This means to literally be their courage; you need to believe in them until they can believe in themselves. You also need to believe in you, even if you don't think anyone else does.

5. Fill your mind with good- What you take in produces what comes out.

6. Keep on keepin on- In the words of the great author Andy Andrews "persist without exception!"

7. Ask for help- Ask for help from people who inspire you, are good at what you want to be good at and who care about you. Also ask for help from God, as He is truly our source of strength. God will do what you can't when you've done what you can. God has opened some incredible doors for me because I was bold enough to ask Him and others for help.

GAME CHANGING MOVES:

1. Take a look at the seven thoughts on building grit, then make a checklist to see where you are succeeding and where you need to make improvements.

2. Watch Dr. Angela Duckworth's Ted Talk on grit via YouTube.

BE AWESOME

Everything is awesome; everything is cool.

Okay, if you have younger children, then you can finish the rest of the sentence above. If you have no clue what I'm talking about, then I need you to go watch the Lego movie and read this chapter when you return. Actually, this chapter has nothing to do with the Lego movie, but it does have something to do with being awesome.

I believe most people desire to be awesome. They want to be excellent in one particular area or maybe many areas of life. But wanting and doing are often divergent roads. As Pastor Steven Furtick, lead pastor of Elevation Church and award winning author put it "We want a calling that we are not willing to commit to." In other words, being awesome sounds great, but putting in work is the true threshing process.

The most successful people I've had the opportunity to be around in life all have one thing in common. They are not afraid to do whatever it takes to fulfill their calling. These people are willing to go the extra mile in order to become the awesome they have conceived in their minds. The highly successful take a concept and then make a commitment to turn the concept into a reality. Let me give you a real-life example.

The young man I will use as my example is Austin Willis. I mentioned Austin and his game changing move in the introduction of this book. I first met Austin when he walked into my locker room to check out football equipment as an 8th grader. He looked athletic, but looks can be deceiving. Then I watched him run during our first practice and was impressed with his speed. After a week of coaching Austin, I knew this young man was special. It wasn't his speed that made him special though; what made Austin special was his work ethic and commitment to becoming great.

Fast forward to the next year and Austin walking into my high school wrestling room to compete for me on the mats. He didn't know much about wrestling at the time, but what he had deep inside made up for his lack of technical knowledge. Over the next four years Austin would earn over 100 wins and over 100 pins as a high school wrestler. He became a multi-time state placer and cemented his legacy on the walls of our wrestling program. That's all cool because people like good stats and can visually see stats on paper, but what they can't see on paper is Austin staying after practice to do extra conditioning. They can't see Austin drilling an extra thirty minutes every day to perfect the system he had developed to beat the people he would face at state. What people can't see is a young man willing to commit to fulfill his calling.

Along with being a successful wrestler, Austin was a high school football standout and track star. Again, these successes were made possible because Austin chose to be about it and not just talk about it. He lived the decision to work toward being awesome. After high school Austin accepted a track scholarship to Emporia State University, a Division 2 school, and walked onto the football team. After a couple years, he focused his efforts toward football and made the commitment to be great in that area of his life.

That decision and all the hard work paid off for Austin. In the fall of 2015 Austin walked on to the football field donning the number 13 on his official Oakland Raiders uniform. He stepped out on the turf and made a fair catch on a punt return, thus completing his first play as an NFL player. Austin had officially become the awesome he conceived in his mind many years ago as a child.

Scott Willis and his son NFL Wide receiver Austin Willis. (2015)

Today I encourage you to commit to the calling you desire. Be willing to work for the awesome you conceive in your mind. It is not easy, but what does that have to do with anything? In the words of the great businessman Charlie Ragus, Founder of AdvoCare International, "If it's easy, we'll do it easy. If it's hard, we'll do it hard." You see, when you are fully committed to your calling, you will follow in the steps of people like Austin Willis and do what it takes to reach your awesome!

GAMES CHANGING MOVES:

1. In what area of life do you want to be awesome? It could be in sports, school, business, parenting, etc. Write that area down and why you chose to be awesome there.

2. What steps do you need to take in order to become awesome in your chosen area? It is a process and will take an immense amount of hard work and dedication.

3. Read 1 Samuel 16:14-23. Notice that David was not only a great warrior, but he was exceptional on the lyre. David was awesome at both because he put in the work, and it paid off as he stood before the king.

PASSION AND ENTHUSIASM

"Light yourself on fire with passion, and people will come from miles to watch you burn." John Wesley

In my mind, there are few characteristics that make a person more attractive than passion. A truly passionate person draws others unto himself and lights a fire that is hard to snuff out.

Recently I had the good fortune of spending a day with one of my closest friends and mentors, Coach Bob Gonzales (aka Gonzo). Gonzo is a long-time school teacher and wrestling coach in Kansas, and he is also one of the most passionate and enthusiastic human beings I've ever met. To say that he is passionate about teaching, coaching and life in general would be a vast understatement.

Coach Robert "Gonzo" Gonzales, Stanford All-American wrestler Tanner Gardner, and Coach Chad Parks. (2008)

After spending the day with Gonzo, I thought about the passion he exudes and how that positively influences everyone around him. I also thought about what each of us can learn from his attitude. Here is a quick breakdown of what comes to mind:

1. He honestly cares for people and expresses it. Gonzo is not afraid to brag on a person in front of everyone else. He doesn't throw out empty words, nor does he hold back praise when it's due.

2. He is a person of action. When something needs to be accomplished, Gonzo gets it done. He does an excellent job of either completing the task himself or delegating it to others. When he finds a person's strong suit, he utilizes that strength and allows the person to shine. Gonzo exemplifies the saying "It doesn't matter who gets the credit as long as the job gets done."

3. He is a servant leader. I can't tell you how many times I've seen this state championship winning coach stay after wrestling practice to wash mops heads, empty trash and pick up the locker room. Gonzo isn't afraid to get his hands dirty completing the seemingly menial task. I know this much; together we have moved more wrestling mats than I'd like to think about. These are the types of servant leader tasks people don't see, but they get done behind the scenes in order to make the machine work. Every great coach I've ever met is a servant leader. This means they not only lead the charge for their team, they are also willing to get in and work themselves.

4. His voice and demeanor carry passion and enthusiasm. To me, this is a trait that can't be faked in a person. You must truly possess passion and enthusiasm for them to exude in you speech and the very manner in which you carry yourself.

I understand every person possesses his or her own unique personality, but I also believe every person can possess great passion and enthusiasm which will then amplify their best personality traits. It is also my humble opinion that every person should strive to acquire and implement the four characteristics listed above into their own life.

Personally, I hope to exemplify passion and enthusiasm in my life the same way my good friend Gonzo does in his. For when you are truly filled with passion and enthusiasm, it spills over and in turn ignites a fire in others.

GAME CHANGING MOVES:

1. Who is the most passionate and enthusiastic person you know? Write down their name and think about how their enthusiasm influences you mentally and emotionally.

2. Take a look at my friend Gonzo's characteristics and think about which of these traits you possess or would like to develop.

3. Watch an Eric Thomas (etthehiphoppreacher) video on YouTube and take in his passion and enthusiasm.

4. What does Colossians 3:23 tells us about how God desires us to go about our work?

PEOPLE ARE WATCHING YOU

People *are* watching you!

Okay, not like Mel Gibson in Conspiracy Theory, but they are watching.

Everything you do in life matters, and it speaks. You may not like it or ask for it, but people are watching you. They are watching your actions, listening to your words and reading what you write (ahem, social media).

You may not believe you are a leader or that what you do has any effect on anyone else. You may be like some of the professional athletes we've seen over the years who act up and then state they are not a role model.

Guess what? If someone is following you, then you are a leader and a role model. That someone might be your son, daughter, relative, friend or teammate. Any or all of these people may be watching your life and trying to figure out how to live their own based on what they see in yours.

Let me make a couple things clear.

I don't believe you should try to impress people. I don't believe other people's opinions about you are any of your business. I don't believe you have to be perfect in life; I mess up all the time, more than I'd like to admit.

That being said, I do believe you need to be the best you can be. You need to do it for you and for the people who are watching you. You need to practice intentional excellence in everything you do because it speaks volumes!

Coach Chad Parks and Carter Hall speaking and presenting at Baccalaureate for the Shawnee Heights High School senior class of 2015.

Look at David in the Bible. Most of us know David killed Goliath and was boosted to national prominence (1 Samuel chapter 17). David was excellent with a slingshot. He was gifted with the sling and intentionally trained for excellence in using it, but did you know David was also gifted on the strings? He intentionally trained for excellence on the lyre, and others were watching him.

King Saul said to his servants "Find someone who can play the lyre well and bring him to me." One of the servants replied "I have seen the son of Jesse who knows how to play the lyre."

Notice the servant didn't even say David's name; he called him the son of Jesse. He might not have known David's name, but he had been watching him. He knew David was a bad dude on the lyre; he could rip up the strings! Based on the servant's word, Saul sent for David. David played the lyre for Saul and Saul liked him so much that he made David one of his armor bearers (1 Samuel 16).

How did David gain the confidence of the king? He practiced intentional excellence, and his life spoke of this fact. People were watching, and they liked what they saw in David.

You never know when someone with your exact skill set is going to be needed by the King. Practice intentional excellence in all areas of your life, and doors you never imagined might open up for you along the way!

GAME CHANGING MOVES:

1. Read 1 Samuel 16 and 17.

2. Did David's actions have any influence on those who were watching him?

3. Who in your life might be watching you? What are they seeing?

4. Do you feel happy or satisfied with what others may see in your example? Why or why not?

LESSONS FROM THE CUSTODIAN

Recently I was standing in my classroom, which is the gym since I teach physical education, and thinking about the retirement of a long-time school custodian. This man's name is Rick Cochran, and he is awesome!

Rick is one of the first faces I see each morning when I arrive to work. Our morning greeting is always the same…

Me: "Good morning Rick."

Rick: "Hey Coach, how's it going?"

This morning pleasantry may seem ordinary, but I assure you it's not. What makes our morning greeting special is not so much the words spoken as it is the person with whom I'm conversing. You see, when Rick greets you, he has a big 'ol smile on his face and a kind voice that conveys to the listener "I care about what you have to say."

I can tell you that I'll miss our morning routine. Beyond the fact that I like the guy, I have also learned from him. Here are five lessons I've learned from Rick over the last 10 years and through his impending retirement:

1. Build relationships. Rick is excellent at building relationships with administration, teachers, paraprofessionals and students. He always takes time to stop, smile and have a meaningful conversation.

2. Take pride in your work. Everything Rick does, he does with pride and excellence. Rick has an exact routine he follows daily. Following the same routine each day could get old and lead to a lackluster performance for some people, but this is not the case for Rick. For example, he cleans the same windows on our gym doors every day and every day they are spotless. This is how Rick performs all his duties. He is a prime example of the saying "The way you do anything is the way you do everything."

3. Exhibit selflessness. Rick absolutely goes out of his way to help others. I can't tell you how often I hear his name called over the intercom to help out someplace in the building. It might be to move a desk, clean a spill or carry boxes dropped off by UPS. Honestly, I don't think any of that matters to Rick; he is willing to help where he is needed.

4. Your job doesn't define you. You can see in Rick it's not so much about the job he is doing as it is about who he is while doing the job. Rick is awesome at his job because he is an awesome person, period. I love this lesson!

5. Leave a legacy of greatness. Someone else will replace you in your job one day. That's the cold hard truth. That being said, leave a legacy of greatness to follow. Rick has performed his job with greatness each and every day. Now he is passing this trait on to his successor. Rick is currently training his replacement and teaching this man the ropes. I have seen the two working together all week and Rick is instructing with the enthusiasm of a first-year school teacher. He is making sure the next man in line is prepared to fill the shoes of a legend.

GAME CHANGING MOVES:

1. Does your job, school or sport define you? Explain why or why not.

2. Who would you be without your job, school, sport, etc.?

3. What kind of legacy do you want to leave in this world? Write out the legacy you'd like to leave at your school, work or with your family.

4. Read 1 Kings 19:19-21. Who does Elijah train up to take his place after him?

DON'T LET OPPORTUNITY PASS YOU BY

The sky is dark and littered with flashes of light as rain hurls itself toward the earth. Local water rising, lakes spilling over and buildings slowly being engulfed by the relentless rise of an unstoppable force. Inside his home a man stands at his window and declares "God will save me." Moments later a neighbor pulls up in his truck and yells "Get in!"

"No, you go ahead... God will save me." Seconds pass by as days and the water will not cease, forcing the man to his rooftop. As he looks to the sky and waits for God to save him, he hears the faint sound of a motor. Out of the heavy rain appears a rescue boat and the occupants shout through the crashing waves "Get in, we are here to help." The man, shaking his head in stubborn contempt, replies back "No, you go ahead. God will save me."

The water is now cresting the rooftop and washing over the man's feet. He is starting to worry and wonder where God is in his time of need. Out of the dark abyss appears a helicopter flying low; it stops directly overhead. Tumbling out of the helicopter drops a basket connected to a rope, landing within the man's reach. The pilot calls down "Climb in the basket and I will pull you to safety. Hurry, there isn't much time." The man shakes his fist at the helicopter and retorts "You get out of here. God will save me."

Calm, peace, light oh so bright. "Sir, wake up and look upon Heaven."

"Wait. What is going on? Why didn't I make it; why didn't God save me?"

"Son, I tried to save you many times. First I sent your neighbor in his truck to drive you to safety, but you refused his help. Next I sent a rescue boat to carry you to higher ground, but you again denied help. At last I sent you a helicopter to fly you to a safe haven, but you rejected the very offer that would change your circumstance." Wow, I love this story.

Below are three lessons about opportunity that can be taken from this wonderful parable.

1. Opportunities often pass by in life because of our stubborn attitudes and preconceived ideas. The man in the story is letting critical opportunities pass him by because he is too hardheaded to take the help right in front of him. We must let go of the pride leading to our slow demise and seize opportunities without reservation.

2. Answers and opportunities don't always come in the form or fashion we expect. Sometimes the very thing we need to change our circumstance is basically smacking us in the face, yet we push it aside in order to look around it for the "perfect" solution. Ask God to open your eyes to the opportunities positioned in front of you right now that you might be overlooking.

3. When opportunities appear, it is our job to take an action step. Many people falter at this point. They might actually recognize an opportunity and believe deep down that it will change their current unpleasant circumstance, but fear grips their mind and they cannot get themselves to take an action step. This ultimately leads to a life of being double minded. To me, that is the scariest place to reside.

Today I encourage you to turn to God with your needs. Ask him to show you which opportunities you need to seize and what attitudes you need to adjust. Finally, ask God to give you the courage to take the action steps necessary to get in the truck, boat or helicopter He's sending your way right now.

GAME CHANGING MOVES:

1. What opportunity has been placed before you at this very moment?

2. Should you seize this opportunity or let it pass by?

3. Do you have any preconceived notions or attitudes that need to be adjusted in order to clearly look at your opportunity?

4. Read Matthew 7:7-8. What does scripture tell us about asking God to help us with our needs?

KEEP YOUR POWER

Not long ago I had a brief discussion with my oldest daughter about methods to deal with situations that upset her. This was a quick conversation but was also one of the most important lessons I've taught her up to this point in her young life.

During school, she had an issue with a friend and it shook her up. That evening at bedtime she was crying while telling her mom all about the situation. Mommy is very good at handling these issues, and I'm normally happy to let her deal with them. I don't really understand girls; I know, big shocker right? This time, though, I felt I needed to share some advice that has helped me deal with various upsetting issues over the years. This little secret works for the young, old, male and female. It covers us all.

I said to my daughter, "can I tell you two actions I take when I start getting upset?" She said yes, and I shared with her the following actions that have helped me time and again:

1. Pray when you feel upset. Ask God to help you, and He'll hear your prayers. There is a wonderful scripture that goes right along with this action...

"I tell you, you can pray for anything, and if you believe that you've received it, it will be yours." -Mark 11:24

2: You must make a decision not to give away your power. You see, when you allow a person or circumstance to upset you, then you give them your power. When you give away your power, that lends itself to anger, fear, frustration, etc. You may not have a choice about what a person says or how a circumstance plays out, but you do have a choice about how you react. The decision is up to you, and God has given us the ability to keep our power instead of giving it away.

"For God has not given us a spirit of fear and timidity, but of power, love, and self-discipline." -2 Timothy 1:7

My daughter seemed to understand my teaching and promised to try this approach next time. It even had an impact on my wife because she later spoke about this event at a high school graduation where she was the guest speaker.

I must admit, utilizing these two actions is not always easy and must be practiced often. The fact is, you can't always control your circumstances, but you can control how you react to them. Today I encourage you to make a decision to keep your power despite your situation. Take action by praying, and then decide you will not give away your power because it comes from God and is a gift to you.

GAME CHANGING MOVES:

1. What situations seem to get you upset and steal your power?

2. Write down the two action steps above and place them in a location where you will see them often.

3. Write down Mark 11:24 and 2 Timothy 1:7. Read these two scriptures daily throughout the next week in order to memorize and internalize the words.

P.R.A.Y.

My wife Laurie is a wonderful human being and a rock-solid foundation in my life. She was a tremendous athlete both in high school and college. After graduating from college, Laurie became an excellent coach and teacher for a number of years at the high school level, but then the Lord placed it upon her heart to become a stay at home mom, devoting her teaching/coaching skills to our four children. To say she excels in this area would be a gross understatement. Laurie is a real-life Wonder Woman!

In saying that, I feel I must share with you a game changing move directly from the brain and heart of my wonder woman. Below are the words from a speech Laurie delivered at a high school baccalaureate ceremony a couple of years ago. It is powerful, and I hope it serves as a game changing move for you, just as it did for so many when first delivered.

Laurie's speech:

Today I am going to share with you an acronym that will help you become successful in life. Would you like to know the secret that will help make you more successful than you can ever imagine? It's an action step you must do daily. And not just daily, but ALL day. Your future depends on it!

That action step is to PRAY!

When I say PRAY, of course I encourage you to pray to God daily or even multiple times per day. However, I would like you to focus on the letters of the word PRAY and what they can mean for your life. Let's take a look.

P= POWER:

My daughter was having difficulties with a few female students in her first-grade class. I went into her room, and I listened to her concerns. After 20 minutes of tears, hugs and encouraging words, I could tell her heart was still aching for direction. I was frustrated because I didn't know what else to say or do. As I left the room, my husband asked if he could talk to her.

Now, I'm sure some of you ladies can relate to what I'm about to say. A conversation with your Mom about "girl drama" is going to be very different than the same topic if discussed with your dad. So, I stood out of sight but close enough I could hear their conversation. Of course, I prayed, "Please Lord, don't let him tell her to just punch the kid in the gut!" As I listened, though, it was quite the opposite.

He told her he was going to share two action steps for her to use in life when dealing with upsetting issues.

Action 1: Pray when you feel upset. Ask God to help you and He'll hear your prayers.

"I tell you, you can pray for anything, and if you believe that you've received it, it will be yours." -Mark 11:24

Action 2: You must make a decision not to give away your power. You see, when you allow a person or circumstance to upset you, you give them your power. When you give away your power, that lends itself to anger, fear and frustration.

"For God has not given us a spirit of fear, but of POWER, love, and self-discipline." -2 Timothy 1:7

Do you want power? How powerful do you want to be?

One of my favorite authors, Andy Andrews, makes reference to power in his book *The Traveler's Gift*, "To do great deeds, great power is essential. Do not run from power. Gather it as you would the finest fruit. Power in the hands of a good person is like a cool drink of water on a hot summer day. It refreshes everyone with whom it comes in contact."

R= RELATIONSHIPS:

Always maintain and grow your relationships. The relationships you have with family, mentors and friends are vital to who you are and who you will become in life.

You will develop new relationships after graduating high school. Be sure these relationships are with people going in the same direction as your faith, your dreams and your goals.

Referring back to *The Traveler's Gift*, Andrews states, "I will choose my friends with care. I am who my friends are. I speak their language and I wear their clothes. I share their opinions and their habits. From this moment forward, I will choose to associate with people whose lives and lifestyles I admire. If I associate with chickens, I will learn to scratch at the ground and squabble over crumbs. If I associate with eagles, I will learn to soar to great heights. I am an eagle. It is my destiny to fly."

We can also read in scripture about the importance of choosing our friends with care.

Proverbs 13:20 tells us:
"Walk with the wise and become wise, for a companion of fools suffers harm."

1 Corinthians 15:33 states:
"Do not be misled. "Bad company corrupts good character."

A= ATTITUDE:

My family loves the song "Happy" by Pharrell Williams. My children love it so much they asked if I could make it my ringtone.
I honestly get excited when my phone rings, because my son's reaction is so awesome. As soon as he hears it, he puffs up his chest, starts to wiggle his head back and forth, and sings "happy, happy, happy." Sometimes I laugh, thinking, "Is he singing along to the song, or attempting a Phil Robertson impression?"

Either way, it brings a smile to my face and pure joy to my heart. Now I realize the song has been overplayed, but I want you to think about the first time you heard it. How did you feel? Did you feel "happy?"

I think most of us will admit that when we heard the song "Happy," we smiled. Do you realize the power of your smile? Take a moment and smile at the person next to you.

What happened when you smiled? Did they smile back? Of course, they did! You have just used your power of influence to brighten their day and make them happy.

Andy Andrews states, "When I choose to smile, I become the master of my emotions. Discouragement, despair, frustration, and fear will always wither when confronted by my smile. The power of who I am is displayed when I smile."

Isaiah 52:7 says,
"How beautiful on the mountains are the feet of those who bring good news, who proclaim peace, who bring good tidings, who proclaim salvation, who say to Zion, "Your God reigns!"

Notice it doesn't say, "Those who complain, those who gossip, those who are negative." It says quite the opposite.

When we choose to have a positive attitude, we are beautiful and we bring our Heavenly Father great joy!

Y= YOUR CREED

If you are going to have a creed, you will need to know what it means. Here is a brief summary of the information I found when researching the word *creed*:

- A statement of shared beliefs of a community and/or religion.
- A summary of core beliefs.
- A set of beliefs that guide someone's actions.

As a child, your parents may have spoken a creed over you, but you didn't realize what it was at the time. For example, every day before school, my dad would pray for me. Then, as soon as I was about to bolt out the door, my mom would grab my hand, kiss me, and say, "Remember who you are and who created you."

Every day, throughout my school years, she would speak this to me. Eventually, as I got older and had a tendency to run late in the mornings, she occasionally had to yell, "Remember who you are and who created you!" as I sprinted out the door.

My children have a creed as well. My husband has taught them a creed that will hopefully be ingrained in their memory for life. It is, "I am a leader. I am a champion. I am blessed By God. Power up!" Then they have a special handshake.

As an adult, my creed is Philippians 4:13, "I can do ALL things through Christ who gives me strength."

It is my battle cry. I use it daily. Sometimes I speak it aloud, sometimes I speak it in my mind or sometimes I even shout it out. I speak it in times of stress and times when I feel like I'm giving away my power. I speak it when making a difficult parenting decision. I speak it when I know I haven't been patient or respectful to my family or friends. I speak it when a negative attitude creeps in. But, most of all, I speak it to God when I don't know what else to say. So, if you ever see me and hear me yell, "I can do all things through

Christ who gives me strength," the appropriate response is not to look at me like I'm crazy or run the other direction. The appropriate response is to follow my creed with, "Amen!"

As you all start this new adventure in your lives, I encourage you to continue to pray and to P.R.A.Y.

Remember, when in doubt, fall into the arms of Jesus. He is your help, and He is your strength.

I leave you with a verse my daughter chose for me to share with you.

Psalm 121:1-2
"I lift up my eyes to the mountains—where does my help come from? My help comes from the Lord, the maker of heaven and earth."

GAME CHANGING MOVES:

1. Where does your power come from, and how can it be maintained?

2. Write down the three most important relationships in your life. Now give thanks and pray for those relationships.

3. How is your attitude most of the time? What can you do to improve your attitude?

4. Choose a scripture that can be used as a creed to help guide your action today and beyond.

THE POWER OF A CREED

Do you have a personal creed? I'm sure you get asked that question a lot. No?

There are a number of uses for the word creed. Some people will associate the word with Apollo Creed from Rocky, Creed the movie, or the video game Assassin's Creed. Here I want to focus on the following definition of the word creed.

Creed- any system or codification of belief or of opinion.

Personally, the word or thought of a creed didn't mean much to me until a few year ago when it suddenly entered my radar. It's kind of funny how it happened too; it was a God thing. My dad and I were hanging out and watching a pastor deliver a message on television. This particular pastor always begins church services with the entire congregation saying a creed in unison. After the parishioners finished saying their creed, my dad says to me "It would be kinda cool to have something like that for your wrestling team." I agreed, but then the notion passed into the land of lost thoughts. Well, at least it seemed that way until the idea found its way back into my mind about six months later.

I was sitting on the couch during Christmas break and typing up the next day's wrestling practice. The same pastor came on the television and bam, the conversation with my Dad popped back into my head. I immediately grabbed a notepad and started writing. I'd guess it was around three minutes later and my wrestling team's creed was officially completed.

That creed I wrote is:

I AM A SHAWNEE HEIGHTS WRESTLER.
STRONGER, FASTER AND BETTER THAN AVERAGE.
TODAY I WILL WORK WITH ALL MY HEART TO IMPROVE
AND PERFECT MY SPORT.
WHEN I STEP ON THE MAT,
I'LL HOLD NOTHING BACK…HOKA HEY!
I AM A SHAWNEE HEIGHTS WRESTLER
AND THIS IS MY DECREE
TO ALWAYS WAH-SKON
AND TCOB!

Big deal, right? Actually yes; it is a big deal. This creed has inspired many, and I believe its impact continues today. In the creed, I placed our team's core beliefs and values. It is the code our wrestlers live by on and off the mats. We even have our own team song, and its basis comes from our creed. Our wrestlers believe in the words written in that creed, and they take a lot of pride in it.

A trickle-down effect, in a good way, is taking place.

I walked into the middle school gym one day, and two of the middle school wrestlers were singing our high school wrestling song. My brain did a couple of back flips inside my head at that very moment. My thought was "YES! These young guys know the song; they are singing it, it's in their head." I knew it was evidence of buy-in to our program. Where did that buy-in start for these young guys? It started with our team creed, tucked beautifully into a rap song.

A few years later I was at a leadership conference and got to listen to a tremendous business leader named Jason Pannell speak. Jason was telling a story about a creed he says with his children each day before they attend school. At that moment, I decided I would write a creed for my children to say as well. Here is the simple creed I wrote for my own children to say:

I am a Leader.
I am a Champion.
I am Blessed by God.

We began saying this creed each night before bed, and it's become a great routine for our family. Well I believe it's great and you know the creed is important to me, but does it matter to my kiddos? The answer can be found in the statement made every time I've tried to sneak out of the bedroom without saying the creed with my children "Dad, we forgot to say the creed." Believe me, I am not allowed to leave the room at bedtime until we have said our creed.

I have good news for you. Creeds aren't just for sports teams or children; they are for you too. If you have a belief system, then you could easily write your own creed. The creed could be for you, your children, your team or your business. The sky's the limit as long as what your write really matters to you and incorporates your belief or value system.

GAME CHANGING MOVES:

1. Create your own creed. You can write it for you, your children, your business, etc. Your creed can be complex, or it can be simplistic. Just write what is on your heart and in your mind.

2. Take your newly written creed and then speak it out loud for the next 30 days. This can take place upon rising, over your lunch break or before bed. Pick a time that works best for you.

3. Read Proverbs 18:21 and Colossians 4:6. What do these scriptures say about the power of the words we speak?

PEBBLE IN YOUR SHOE

"It isn't the mountains ahead to climb that wear you out; it's the pebble in your shoe." Muhammad Ali

The modest things in life matter more than most people realize. Small disciplines repeated daily can lead to great success in various areas of your life. On the flip side, these small disciplines neglected daily can lead to epic failure.

Let me share an example with you from my own life. I know without a doubt my day runs smoother if I get up in the morning and complete the following tasks: pray, write in my gratitude journal and read my daily devotional.

These are three simple tasks that when completed each morning get my mind moving in the right direction. They are small disciplines that make a big impact on my day. Yet I often wake up, let laziness take over, then forego writing in my gratitude journal or reading my devotional. I usually squeeze a quick prayer in there even though it's often thought-less. If I'm not careful, I'll look up and three days have passed where I haven't completed the basic practice I know benefits me in all areas of my life. When that happens, it affects my personal attitude and that spreads amongst my household. I'm certain my wife would attest to this if you ask her.

I empathize with the Apostle Paul's sentiment in Romans 7:15 when he says "I don't really understand myself, for I want to do what is right, but I don't do it. Instead, I do what I hate." I feel you Paul; the struggle is real.

Now let me ask you a simple, yet relevant, question. What seemingly small disciplines do you need to focus on each day to become the best you possible? Small disciplines completed consistently influence everything you do in life. They can be a deciding factor between success or failure in sports, school, business, parenting and more. These seemingly minute actions can allow you to reach your full potential or keep you living in a state of stagnation.

Do you have a mountain to scale but you can't seem to gain traction in climbing toward the top? Well, it might be the pebble in your shoe that's holding you back. If this is the case, then decide today you will take care of the small disciplines in order to succeed in life's big tasks.

GAME CHANGING MOVES:

1. Write down 2-3 areas where you really want to see growth in your life. These can be in sports, fitness, business, your faith life, etc.

2. Look at your 2-3 areas of growth and write down 1-2 small disciplines you can complete daily in each area of concentration.

3. Start with making your bed. This is one simple habit you can control and accomplish quickly. When you add a habit, it's easy to add another on top of it, also known as stacking. An example is make your bed daily and then complete 50 push-ups immediately after. This is akin to killing two birds with one stone.

4. Read Song of Solomon 2:15. What do the foxes have to do with small disciplines?

SMALL TOWN VALUES

I grew up in a one-horse town. Okay, actually it has a lot of horses, but only one stop light. When I was a kid that stoplight had three colors. Today it just flashes red. I'm not sure where green and yellow went.

Anyway, I love that one stoplight town. That area of Oklahoma is called "Green Country," but we call it "God's Country." This is just a gut feeling, but I think God calls it that too.

Laurie Parks, Kate Parks, Ally Parks, and Chad Parks walking in downtown Pawhuska, OK. (2010)

There are so many awesome things I can write about my hometown of Pawhuska, OK. However, what I am writing about today is not so much the town as it is the values I learned growing up there. These values are not exclusive to Pawhuska or small towns in general, but these are values I learned growing up in a small town and still try to employ in my life today, even while living in a large city.

Here are a few values commonly observed in small towns:

People wave at you. I know that's weird. I have lived in a large city long enough that I forget about waving at people, especially when driving. Then I pass through a small town or visit back home and get caught off guard. You know the situation. You are driving down the road, someone passes by and they wave as they pass. You see the wave but it's too late to react. You try to get in a quick wave, but you know they didn't see your return wave. I'm kind of glad we don't wave in the city though; there are a lot of people and that would get exhausting. That being said, I miss the friendliness of a good ole wave.

Shaking hands. People in small towns still shake your hand as a greeting, parting gesture or to seal a deal. This is a part of life all people, especially men, should hold in high regard.

The use of Sir or Ma'am. People in small towns often say "Yes, Sir or Yes, Ma'am." These terms are used when addressing those you respect, especially your elders. Personally, I highly respect people who use these terms when speaking to others.

Opening doors for women and elders. It is a common practice in small towns to hold open the door for women or anyone who is your elder. Not only holding open doors, but opening car doors as well. My daughters will not date a guy who doesn't open the door for them when they are old enough to date at the age of 21.

Taking off your hat indoors. It is a sign of respect to take off your hat indoors. This is especially true when entering a person's house, a restaurant or a church.

Respecting elders. This includes many of the acts mentioned above and more, like moving over on the sidewalk to let an elder walk by, listening when an elder talks to you without interrupting them, and helping with anything you see they might need help with on a daily basis. This could include putting away groceries, crossing the street, or taking the newspaper up to their front door from the driveway. Last but not least, you always clean the snow off the driveway for an elder who might have trouble doing it themselves.

Those are just a few of the values I learned growing up in "God's Country." I know these values have helped me succeed in many areas of my life. They are also lessons I teach to my children, athletes and others with whom I have influence. Overall, these values are about being good to people, and that goes a long way in every area of life.

GAME CHANGING MOVES:

1. Write down 4-5 values you admire and adhere to on a regular basis.

2. What values do you need to work on in order to become more consistent in being good to people?

3. Pick one small town value and put it into practice starting today.

4. Read Luke 6:31 and Galatians 5:14. What do these scriptures teach you about how we should treat others?

LISTEN AND LEARN

Last summer I had the opportunity to listen to and absorb wisdom from one of my elders and a man I admire, Vann Bighorse, Elder in the Osage Nation and Osage language expert. I'm only sharing a small portion of what Vann said, but I feel it is of the utmost importance. Vann's message was this, "No matter how young or old you are, you must keep learning. You must keep learning until the day you move on to that other side. In this manner, you are like a young person, regardless of your current age; a young person learning from your elders and those who have come before you."

When your elders are speaking, you need to listen. Listen to their wisdom so you may be able to apply it in your own life."

In my opinion, this is a lesson we all need to hear and implement into our lives. Thankfully there are many wise people out there willing to teach, train and mentor us. There are people who have acquired years upon years of knowledge, which has become wisdom, and they will happily share it with us. These people have paved the way for our generation, and we must not take that lightly.

The way I see it, the key is this.

We must be willing to stop, really listen to our elders speak, and then learn from the knowledge they have acquired through the years. When I say learn, it's not just head knowledge. We must obtain the head knowledge, then connect it with our hearts and apply it in our lives.

I'm so thankful for all the wonderful people God has placed in my life from whom I can learn. Men like Vann Bighorse who listened to his elders and is now passing on that knowledge and wisdom to others. The truth is, before each of us knows it, we will be one of the elders passing on knowledge and wisdom to the next generation.

GAME CHANGING MOVES:

1. Write down a few elders in your life from whom you can learn. These people could be parents, grandparents, coaches, teachers, etc. Make a plan to visit them and gather as much wisdom as possible. Ask questions and then really listen to what they have to share.

2. Visit a nursing home and hang out with a few of the residents. When you leave, journal how you feel personally and how you think the people you just visited feel about spending time with you.

3. Read James 1:19. How often do you follow this Biblical principle?

4. Read 1 Peter 5:5 and Timothy 5:1-3. What does scripture have to say about respecting elders?

FORGIVENESS

Yesterday my toddler son was doing what toddlers do, get into everything!

I walked into the kitchen and found my little man eating candy from a bag his sisters had brought home from a birthday party. I took the bag from my son and told him, "no no." He looked at me with that "dang it man, I got caught" look in his eyes.

About an hour later I walked into the living room and there was my son holding two more bags of candy, about to sneak down the stairs to the basement. Our eyes met, and he knew trouble was in the air. I told him "put the bags down right now!" He looked at me, looked at the stairs, then sat his bottom at the top of the stairs and went sliding down as fast as he could go.

I took off down the stairs to retrieve the candy and take my son to his room for a time out. When I snatched him up, he started crying and saying 'no.' Part of those tears were because he was in trouble, but the tears were mostly shed because he just lost the candy!

Later that week I was sitting in church and the whole candy scenario popped into my mind. I had a revelation about the situation that struck a chord in my heart. I realized I am a lot like my two-year-old son. How? Well, I often do whatever I want to do and easily give in to temptation. Sometimes I even look God in the eyes and know that what I'm about to do is wrong. Then just like my little boy, I quickly do the wrong anyway because I'm selfish and want things done my way.

After I realized my son and I aren't that different in our daily actions, another revelation sped into my brain. You see, even though my son disobeyed and got into trouble for doing wrong, I quickly forgave him. I forgave him and also loved him, regardless of his actions. This is what God does this with us, He forgives and loves us regardless of our actions. His love for us cannot be broken by our own selfish behavior and wrongdoings.

In Romans 8:38-39 Paul says: "And I am convinced that nothing can ever separate us from God's love. Neither death nor life, neither angels nor demons, neither our fears for today nor our worries about tomorrow—not even the powers of hell can separate us from God's love. No power in the sky above or in the earth below—indeed, nothing in all creation will ever be able to separate us from the love of God that is revealed in Christ Jesus our Lord."

So today if someone around you messes up, be quick to forgive and quick to show them love. Holding a grudge or unforgiveness in your heart will keep you from becoming the person God intends you to be. It will halt your progress in reaching your true potential in every area of your life. They say harboring unforgiveness is like drinking poison and expecting the other person to be affected by it. On a personal level, when you mess up, know that you have a loving heavenly father who forgives you completely and loves you more than you could ever imagine. He sent His Son to prove it. P.S. There was one more learning point in this whole situation with my son. After he was finished with his time out, he ran over and said "Daddy, hold you?" This is what he says when he wants me to hold him. So, I picked him up and we hugged for a little while. We need to be like my little boy and run to God when we mess up. God will pick us up in His strong arms and give us the comfort we need to know it's all going to be okay.

GAME CHANGING MOVES:

1. Review your life and decide if there is someone you need to forgive. Remember, forgiveness isn't about them; it's a choice for you.

2. Is there anyone you need ask forgiveness from because you messed up? Step up, reach out, and ask this person to forgive you.

3. Read Matthew 27:32-56. What does Jesus example on the cross teach you about forgiveness?

4. What is the difference between forgiving someone for a wrong and letting that person take advantage of you time and again?

BEND DON'T
BREAK

When I was around 14 or 15 years old we had a horrible storm move through my hometown of Pawhuska, OK. I grew up tornado alley, so a strong storm was nothing out of the ordinary for us Okies, but this particular storm was one like I had never seen. This storm contained straight line winds that blew over 100 mph, and it looked as if it were raining sideways. I had never experienced straight line winds of that magnitude and was a little freaked out, to be honest.

Earlier that day I had been out cutting grass, but the rain moved in and shut me down. So, I went home, put away my mowing equipment and walked into the house. Minutes later I heard the wind howling and ran to the kitchen window just in time to see part of our backyard wooden fence go flying across the yard. The sideways rain was impeding my view, so I decided to move to the front window and see if the view was clearer on that side of the house.

All I could see was the rain blowing sideways at first, but then I could vaguely make out my neighbor's house and their front yard. Our neighbors had the most incredibly landscaped yard, filled with beautiful trees, bushes, flowers, etc. My eyes caught movement just in time to see one of their magnificent trees crack under the pressure and power of the straight-line wind. The old and mighty tree put up a good fight, but eventually tumbled to the ground, leaving only a jagged stump behind as a sign of its existence.

Suddenly, it was as if the storm slowed in my mind and I could only focus on one singular item, a tree in the middle of my neighbor's yard (my favorite of all their trees). The tree was bent over sideways, but even with the pressure of the substantial winds, it was not breaking. Everything around this tree was in trouble, but somehow it was able to bend but not break.

Today I want this story to encourage you and maybe even bring about a revelation in your heart and mind. Sometimes life will throw unexpected storms at you. Everything around you may seem out of control, breaking and falling apart under the impending pressure, but the key is to be like my neighbor's tree that withstood the power of the storm. Make no mistake, this tree did not stand mighty and unscathed by the storm coming against it. However, it wasn't broken by the storm either. It bent to what seemed to be its limit and the impending outcome did not look good, but the tree fought against the odds and was able to bend but not break.
So, when life's storms hit and you feel as if you are at your limit, remember that like the tree, you can bend but not break!

GAMES CHANGING MOVES:

1. When was the last time you went through a storm in your life?

2. Write down one or two lessons from the personal storm.

3. Congratulations, you are reading this and that means you are still here. The storm did not break you. Write down a list of things you are grateful for at this very moment.

4. Read Luke 8:23. How does this story relate to life's storms and the ability to make it through them without breaking?

COOL KIDS

Education and athletics are wonderful places for our youth to learn about various educational topics and life in general. Along with all the transference and acquisition of knowledge that takes place, there is also a great amount of social engagement occurring. This is where I want to land for this chapter, right smack dab in the middle of social cultivation.

I have been a middle school teacher and a high school coach for a number of years. I'm also the parent of two elementary students and two toddlers. What I'm getting at is that I get to see the social matrix from top to bottom. Besides that, I've personally experienced all these levels and currently reside in the adult level of the social matrix.

No matter where you are in life, the same social issue exists. What is this issue? It is the idea of the haves and have nots, the cool kids and the not so cool kids.

Some of you read that last sentence and thought, "hey, I was a cool kid back in the day!" Let it go, let it go. Others of you read the cool kids statement and were taken back to a time and place you'd like to forget. Maybe many of you have experienced both sides of the coin. In most school systems (I'd guess 100 percent of them) there are groupings or cliques of young people that have similar interests. You can often pick out these cliques based on clothing, speech, activities, etc. Being with others who have similar interests is not bad;

it's normal human behavior. However, when these cliques of people begin to develop a social class system, then we have issues.

So, let me get down to the nitty gritty, as I'm not one to mince words. What truly concerns me more than anything else with social cliques in the school social structure is not the clique, but the attitudes of the people therein. I'm actually talking about the attitude of every individual person, as you can only control your own attitude and not that of others. No matter what group you feel you belong to or what label you have been given, this is the truth, your attitude matters.

Therefore, it is imperative you never let anyone make you feel 'less than' in life. You control your attitude, so choose to make it a good one. Choose to be upbeat, positive, and to place a smile on your face. Today is the day to stop worrying about your status and living life to impress others. You must choose to live your life in such a way that you are focused on being the best you possible. You must also live your life in such a way that you boost others and help them to become the best they can be as well.

Don't spend one more day trying to fit in with the "cool kids" or any other group of people, for that matter. You be you, because in reality, that's all you can be anyway. If you spend every day becoming a "cool you," then you will naturally attract others to you. If for some reason someone doesn't like you or you don't fit into their group, it's their loss. You be you baby because you are unique; you are awesome; and you matter!

Adults, this message is for you too. Many times, adults can be just as guilty of social cliques as school kids. It's time to stop trying to keep up with the Jones and start being you. You control your attitude, so go to work on becoming the best you, because you are unique; you are awesome; and you matter! Beyond that, you are setting an example for your children to follow. What matters more than that?

Coach Justin Vest, Wrestler Brett Yeagley, and Coach Chad Parks
at the Class 5A Kansas High School state wrestling tournament. (2016)

GAME CHANGING MOVES:

1. Ask yourself this question "Am I trying to fit in, or do I focus on becoming the best version of me?"

2. Write down a time in your life when you were "cool" and write down a time when you were an "outcast."

3. Did either of these times influence who you are today as a human being? If so, how?

4. Read Psalm 119:73-74 and Isaiah 64:8. What do these scriptures say about who you are as a person?

DO YOU EVEN LIFT?

You may or may not have heard this phrase "Bro, do you even lift?" It has become a funny punch line, has inspired comical YouTube videos, and is even printed on T-shirts. Basically, it's a way to tease people who are in good shape, maybe too muscled up, or are "fitness experts."

I have to admit the line is getting old, but I still find it funny. I am a coach, athlete and workout freak, so the phrase applies to my life in the comical sense.

With that being said, this chapter is not about lifting weights at all. It's about lifting people. Not like a cheerleader lifts someone over their head, but as in lifting people's spirits.

We have this incredible power to use our words and actions to lift others. One kind word can change someone's day or even life. Your smile might be all the action needed to lift the spirit of someone who feels like no one cares. Positive psychology research has shown that even the smallest positive gestures can increase happiness and lift one's spirit. On the contrary, science has shown that negative words actually influence the same area of the brain that activates when we receive a physical injury. The old saying "Sticks and stones might break my bones, but words will never hurt me" has now been proven false.

We should always look for ways to encourage, not discourage. We should build people up, not tear them down. We should be on the lookout for ways to lift people with our words and actions. As a coach this is vitally important to the athletes I train and how they view themselves in sports and as people. The same goes for my role as a parent. It's easy to get frustrated and use negative words with my children, but ultimately this shapes who they will become as adults. There are many adults today who say, "I was raised that way and I'm fine. It just made me tougher than most people." Yet these same people are carrying around years and years of emotional baggage because the adults in their life beat them down verbally.

So today I encourage you to start lifting. Lift people up at times when they might be sad or lonely. Lift them up when they do right and speak life into their hearts when they need a helping hand. Before you know it, you will be a great encourager and life lifting words will flow out of your mouth as naturally as water from a spring.

My question for you is this... "Bro, do you even lift?"

GAME CHANGING MOVES:

1. Read Proverbs 16:24. Does this sound like the kind of words you speak on a regular basis?

2. Ancient wisdom says life and death are in the tongue. What is your tongue bringing you these days, life or death?

3. Who do you know that often speaks negative, bone breaking words? Who do you know that speaks life giving words? Which do you find more motivational?

4. Journal each night before you go to bed, writing down some uplifting scriptures from the Bible. Then speak those words aloud and watch them get into your innermost being, changing you from the inside out.

YOUR MENTAL FORECAST

Did you know your mind has its own atmosphere? And did you realize the atmosphere of your mind can control how you feel mentally, physically and spiritually? Furthermore, did you know you can control the atmosphere of your mind?

You see, what you take in daily directly affects what is going on in your head. Let me ask you some questions and make some connections here so that this thought process makes sense.

What are you taking in daily through your eyes and ears? Do you wake up and watch one of the 24-hour news stations? What do these stations show all day long? Death, destruction, fear, conflict, etc.

What television shows and or movies do you watch each week? How about the music scene; what are you listening to in the car or at home?

Do you wake up and read social media sites such as Facebook or Twitter before you even go to the bathroom in the morning? This may not be bad in and of itself, but it depends who, and what you follow. Do you have Facebook friends who constantly post radical news, depressing posts, drama, or all around negativity? Is your twitter feed filled with good or bad? By the way, you don't have to read all of the articles being posted; the headlines can be enough to get your mind going in the right direction or the wrong one.

Who are you hanging around all day? Where and with whom do you spend your free time in the evenings or the weekends? Okay, I think that about covers the gamut. The point is that each of the areas listed above helps propagate the atmosphere in your mind. When you take in fear, negativity, depression, and drama then guess what's running rampant in your mind? Guess who you are letting rent space and create a nasty atmosphere in your brain? That's right; you are letting fear, negativity, depression and drama rent space in your mind and corrupt your mental atmosphere. Now let's look at the other side of the coin and see how to create a good atmosphere in your mind. In my opinion, the first place to start is in the book containing the greatest wisdom known to man, the Bible.

The Bible says in Philippians 4:8 "Finally, brothers and sisters, whatever is true, whatever is noble, whatever is right, whatever is pure, whatever is lovely, whatever is admirable--if anything is excellent or praiseworthy--think about such things."

When you think about things that are true, noble, right, pure, lovely and admirable, then guess what kind of atmosphere is being created in your mind? That's easy… a good one.

When you are filling your brain with good thoughts from positive books, music, television shows and people, then the outcome will be a positive atmosphere in your head.

Here is one important piece of information I feel is critical in this line of thinking; you must create the right atmosphere in your head on a daily basis. You can't do it once in a while and expect to have a great mental atmosphere. It is literally a daily practice.

When you wake up in the morning, that's the time to get going in the right direction, but morning is just the start and you'll need to be aware of and intentional about what you are taking in all day long. I know what you are thinking now, and you are right; this isn't easy.

If it was easy, then everyone would do it. What is easy is just simply being. What is easy is letting any old thought land in your mind and free load as long as it wants. Yet it is imperative to realize that this easy route leads to a dark atmosphere that takes your mind to places you don't want to go. So, you must be willing to do your part in creating the best atmosphere possible through intentional actions and thinking.

Today I encourage you to be 100 percent honest with yourself about what you are letting into your mind. Then ask yourself if what you are letting in is creating the atmosphere you want in your brain and is it making you the person you desire to become in life? I know for me, I have to get honest with myself a lot and force myself to refocus on what I need to do to improve my mental atmosphere every day.

Now let me go back to Philippians 4:8. "Finally, brothers and sisters, whatever is true, whatever is noble, whatever is right, whatever is pure, whatever is lovely, whatever is admirable--if anything is excellent or praiseworthy--think about such things."

Do you know what Scripture precedes Philippians 4:8? Verses 1-7? Yes, but check out what it says in Philippians 4:6-7 "Do not be anxious about anything, but in every situation, by prayer and petition, with thanksgiving, present your requests to God. And the peace of God, which transcends all understanding, will guard your hearts and your minds in Christ Jesus."

I point out these two verses because they directly correlate with your mental atmosphere. You see, in every situation you are to pray to God with thanksgiving and He will give you peace while also guarding your heart and mind in Christ. Then, think about the good things stated in Philippians 4:8. When you do this, you create a good atmosphere in your mind and ultimately your mental atmosphere creates your world.

Six simple real life steps to take in creating a great mental atmosphere:

1. Pray.
2. Read your Bible.
3. Hang out with people who inspire, uplift and help you in life.

4. Don't watch junk on television or the videos on the internet.
5. If someone posts negative, drama, etc. on Facebook or Twitter, unfollow them. You're a big person, and you can control what you want to see on your social media sites. It doesn't mean you don't like the person; it means you are being responsible for you.
6. Take in good through people, books, music, television and media that inspires you and creates the mental atmosphere you want.

GAME CHANGING MOVES:

1. What actions do you take in order to create a great mental atmosphere? Write out your thoughts.

2. Journal your feelings at the end of each day, then reflect back to see if what you brought into your mind influenced your mental state for the positive or negative.

3. Read Philippians 4:6-8. How does this scripture make you feel?

NOT QUALIFIED

It is funny how life can take unexpected twists, and God can lead you into places you'd never dream up on your own. I have seen this in my own life, and I'm sure many of you have as well.

I want to tell you a story about my Great Grandfather, Charley H. Parks. You see, Charley Parks' journey took a twist that not only changed his life forever but also the lives of countless others around the world.

In 1929 Charley was a pumper in the oil fields of Oklahoma and a part time cowboy. One particular day he had an accident while breaking a horse for a local rancher that led to him breaking his ankle. Well, working in the oil fields and on ranches with a broken ankle wasn't easy, but the work wasn't going to do itself. Charley had a family to feed, and that meant he had to work and earn money whether healthy or injured.

Before I continue, let me interject with some information about Charley Parks. According to local legends, Charley was one tough man. He was 6'5" and made of pure muscle. His hands were gigantic, which came in handy for manual labor and also for putting a whooping on other men when the need arose. Yep, they say Ole Charley didn't mind getting into a scuffle every now and then, and he was pretty good at it. If you know any members of the Parks family before they find Jesus, then this sounds about right.

Early one morning Charley went out to check one of his oil leases, walking by an old water well on the way to his lease. As he passed the well, he heard a voice say "Charley go kick the water well." He looked back to see who was talking to him, but there was no one around. So, he continued on down to check his lease. On the way back Charley passed the well and again heard a voice say "Charley go kick the water well." He looked around and didn't see a soul anywhere. Then the voice said "Charley, go kick the water well and I'll heal your ankle."

Charley walked over to the water well and kicked it, but nothing happened. So, he kicked it again, still nothing. This time he reared back and really gave the well a good kick. Bam! Every bone in his ankle snapped back into place, and the pain subsided. When Charley arrived home, he took off his boots and to his amazement, there was no longer any swelling, bruising or pain. His ankle was healed, just as the voice said it would be.

Charley then turned his eyes toward the sky and dedicated his life to the Lord. He knew at that very moment he was called to do more than work in the oil fields and be a cowboy. Charley felt deep down in his heart that he was called to be a preacher of the Gospel. So that's just what he did, but this decision wasn't made without first fighting it out with God.

You see, Charley had no education and therefore couldn't read. So how was he supposed to become a preacher when he couldn't even read his Bible? There was also opposition from his lovely bride who proclaimed "I married a cowboy, not a preacher." If these issues weren't large enough, the great depression was starting up in America and money was in short supply. At this time, a man didn't just walk away from his job and become a preacher without a guaranteed source of income to feed his family.

Charley was not qualified to become a preacher, and all the odds were stacked against him. So, guess what he did? Yep, he became a preacher. He knew in his heart this was his calling and that if God called him to do it, then He'd make a way.

Charley Parks went on to preach for the next 63 years of his life. He had the opportunity to preach all over America and help lead many to the Lord. Charley was not only good at oil field and ranch work; he was a terrific carpenter. This skill came in handy as Charley would build a church in almost every community where he lived and preached. He would move to a town, build the church and then build "the church." He also built houses for many people in the local congregation and those who needed a place to live.

My great grandpa Charley Parks, also known as Chod or Brother Parks, was an amazing man. He lived an incredible life and our family is still being blessed today because of his dedication to the Lord, but here is what I want to share with you about his awesome story.

You don't have to be qualified for God to use you, but when life throws you a twist and God comes calling, you must answer! You need not worry about the "how," you need only to say "Here I am Lord, use me now."

God is an expert at taking men and women who are under qualified and using them to expand His kingdom. The Bible is filled with these stories from Moses to the Disciples. The key is to be willing to lay down your guard and open your heart to the Lord, then God will equip you with everything you need to do his will and more. Today, I encourage you, like Charley Parks, to look toward the sky and dedicate your life to the Lord. Then be willing to let God use you in ways you may have never dreamt or imagined. It might be difficult going from cowboy to preacher, but God's plan is the only place any of us will ever be right at home here on this earth. His will is the only way we will ever be all we can be for Him, us and the people who cross our paths.

One time my dad asked Grandpa Parks "How is it that you can read your Bible, but you can't read the newspaper?" Grandpa just looked at my dad and said "I don't know, but I do know that when I read my Bible, the words light up and I can understand them. This doesn't happen when I read anything else."

GAME CHANGING MOVES:

1. When was the last time you pursued something you didn't feel qualified for? Did you pursue it anyway?

2. What is your vision for the future about who God is calling you to be? Write it down and pray about it.

3. Read *(Un)Qualified* by Steven Furtick.

4. Read Luke 5:1-11. Do you think Jesus' new disciples qualified as religious leaders according to the religious elites of that time?

BE ABOUT IT

I believe in the power of words and the effect they have on a person's life. Along with words, I believe in action.

Action is not always easy to come by these days. Plenty of people give lip service, but they don't back that up by putting their shoe leather to the road. In other words, they don't do what they say they are going to do. I mean, everyone wants to have success, get the win and earn great money, but not everyone is willing to take the actions steps necessary to reach those milestones.

Let's look at an example of lip service and shoe leather given by Jesus as recorded in the book of Matthew, often referred to as The Parable of the Two Sons.

"What do you think? There was a man who had two sons. He went to the first and said, 'Son, go and work today in the vineyard.'
"'I will not,' he answered, but later he changed his mind and went.
"Then the father went to the other son and said the same thing. He answered, 'I will, sir,' but he did not go.

"Which of the two did what his father wanted?"

"The first," they answered.

What an excellent story. One son says he's not in, but he gets it done anyway. The other son says 'I got this,' but he doesn't come through. People don't always believe what you say, but they will believe what you do!

Here is an excellent parable I recently heard from my pastor about lip service and action. Our pastor was actually using this story as an illustration for faith, but it works well for action too. The story goes as follows.

There was a man very skilled in his craft, which happened to be walking across tightropes. Not just any tightrope either, but extreme tightrope walking. On one occasion this tightrope expert was attempting to cross the Grand Canyon. As crowds gathered, the anticipation was palpable. The tightrope walker bravely stepped out onto the rope and began his journey to the other side of the canyon. With every step the crowd held its breath in one accord, full of anticipation, excitement and a little fear.

Slowly but surely the tightrope walker crossed over to the opposing side of the Grand Canyon and stepped onto land. All the people gathered around and cheered in amazement at this incredible accomplishment. The star of the moment made a motion for the crowd to hush and listen to his words. It was at this point he said, "Would you like to see more?" The crowd again burst forth with awe and excitement. The tightrope walker hushed the crowd once more and declared, "This time I will attempt to cross back over the Grand Canyon, but I will not go it alone. I shall push a wheelbarrow filled with dirt along the tightrope as I cross back to the side where I originally began."

The people went wild and shouted encouragement to this brave soul who dared to defeat gravity and the Grand Canyon once again. One last time the tightrope walker spoke to the crowd, "Do you think I can do it?" "Yes, Yes, Yes," they shouted with confidence and encouragement. "Well then," said the tightrope walker as he dumped out the dirt from the wheelbarrow onto the ground. "Since you are all so sure I will succeed, who will get into the wheelbarrow and go with me?"

Crickets.

You see, it is easy to talk about doing something great, but actually taking action is an entire different level of commitment. It's easy to dare greatly in words but not so much in doing.

Today I encourage you to speak words that have a wonderful effect on your life, but I also encourage you to back these words up with action. In short, don't just talk about it; be about it.

GAME CHANGING MOVES:

1. What areas of your life have you been talking about taking action but have only procrastinated to this point?

2. What happens to you mentally when you finally take action on something you've been putting off?

3. Do you know anyone who does not do what they say they are going to do? How does that make you feel?

4. Read James 2:14-26 and ponder James' words concerning faith and action.

ACTION > FEAR

"For the Spirit God gave us does not make us timid, but gives us power, love and self-discipline." 2 Timothy 1:7

If you are human, you've dealt with fear at some point in your life. Certain fears aren't bad and are built in to help protect you, but even at that, I don't know if it's so much a fear as it is a healthy respect for that which presents danger. Let's look at snakes for an example. I'm not really fearful of snakes, but I do have a healthy respect for snakes and understand that a snake bite could be bad business.

What I am talking about is the fear that seizes and locks you up. The fear that creeps into your mind and keeps you from getting out of your comfort zone and being all that you can become in life. The fear that wakes you at 5 a.m. and starts overwhelming you with thoughts about all that you must do in the coming year.

So, fear happens. What can you do about it?

Take action!

That's what you can do about fear, take action. Sitting around frozen doesn't do you any good unless you work for Disney (see what I did there, *Frozen*.) Avoiding your better future because of fear is just a stupid idea and you know it. Helen Keller hit the nail on the head when she said,

"Avoiding danger is no safer in the long run than outright exposure. The fearful are caught as often as the bold."

The decision to act allows you to take a bold approach, and the result is a dissipation of fear. Action doesn't always allow you to completely conquer fear, but it does let you know that you have the power to do what needs to be done.

Even though I grew up painting houses and have been on some really tall ladders in precarious situations, I still have a fear of heights. I have attempted to stomp out this fear for good by participating in some extreme skyward adventures, but they didn't cure me. What they did do is let me know I can control my mind and beat back the fear when I want to do so.

Action allows you to be bold, look fear in the eyes, then throw it on its head. There is a lot of mental, spiritual and physical freedom in taking on fear and beating it down. Inaction, on the other hand, wrecks your confidence and breeds more fear. It leaves you scared, confused and full of doubt. World renown author Dale Carnegie said it this way "Inaction breeds doubt and fear. Action breeds confidence and courage. If you want to conquer fear, do not sit home and think about it. Go out and get busy."

Today I encourage you to stop letting fear control your life. Even if you don't know what to do, do something! Step out of your comfort zone and take action. This is the road to becoming the person God has planned for you to become. Take action starting today, and watch your fears dissipate.

It's amazing how fear can appear as an impenetrable wall blocking your way. Yet when you take courage and walk toward that wall, you find it's only a vapor quickly vanishing without a trace.

GAME CHANGING MOVES:

1. Write down your top three fears right now.

2. Write down 2-3 actions you can take over the next month to help you deal with these fears.

3. Read Ephesians 6:1-20. How do these words and the imagery provided by them make you feel about taking fear head on?

4. Read *Start: Punch Fear in the Face* by Jon Acuff.

THREE BIRDS ON A WIRE

Three birds are sitting on a wire and one of them decides to fly away; how many birds are left? If you guessed two, then you are incorrect. There are still three birds sitting on a wire at this time. Wait, what?

I know right now you are questioning my mathematical abilities, but let me explain. If you read the opening sentence again you'll notice I didn't say that one of the birds flew away; I said it decided to fly away. There is a big difference between deciding to do something and actually doing it. Intent and action are not the same, even though many people gauge themselves by their intentions rather than their actions. In this case, the bird that decided to fly away is no different than the other two birds who never intended to move at all.

Let's say one of the wrestlers I coach decides he wants to be the best wrestler in the state at his weight class. He tells me he intends to compete in our freestyle wrestling program, attend summer wrestling camp, and lift weights throughout the off season. But life happens, and this wrestler ends up only attending a couple of freestyle wrestling practices, misses wrestling camp because he has another commitment, and never finds the weight room due to a hectic lifeguarding schedule at the lake.

Did this wrestler improve because he "decided" to pursue all of his wrestling options in the off season? The answer is a definitive no, because his intentions did not line up with his actions. Overall, he is no better off than the wrestler who never intended to work out in the off season to begin with. They are both sitting on the same wire watching life pass them by.

Now apply this thought process of intention versus action to your own life. You have made a decision to start getting in shape this year, but that couch is calling your name every evening. You are intending to buy your wife flowers and take her on a date, yet you just can't find the extra time since you return home from the office so late. You will get that Plan B business off the ground as soon as this next holiday is finished and you have more time to focus on it.

You see, great intentions in and of themselves have no actual power or value. The best decisions running through your mind are really dry creek beds without movement. You must first make a decision, and that is undoubtedly important, but more important is putting action behind that decision and turning intentions into realities.

Today I encourage you to evaluate a few areas of your life where your intentions are not matching up with your actions, then be bold enough to take the first steps into action right now. Don't wait any longer because life's too short and your contribution to it is of the utmost importance to everyone around you. You owe it to yourself and others to make a decision to fly and then actually take to the air!

GAME CHANGING MOVES:

1. Pick one area of your life where you need to move from intent into action. Write down that area, along with three action steps you can take right now to get started.

2. Ask yourself, "Do you gauge yourself by your intentions but judge others by their actions?" The two need to line up.

3. Who do you know that is a person of decision and action? Call, text, or email them to get some pointers on how to get going in your own life. There are very few original ideas; do what successful people do.

"Dear friends, do you think you'll get anywhere in this if you learn all the right words but never do anything? Does merely talking about faith indicate that a person really has it? For instance, you come upon an old friend dressed in rags and half-starved and say, "Good morning, friend! Be clothed in Christ! Be filled with the Holy Spirit!" and walk off without providing so much as a coat or a cup of soup—where does that get you? Isn't it obvious that God-talk without God-acts is outrageous nonsense?" - James 2:14-17

WISDOM FROM UNCLE ED

Years ago, when I was just a young man, my dad and I were talking with a highly-respected Elder of the Osage Nation. This man's name was Ed Red Eagle Sr., but we called him Uncle Ed.

Uncle Ed was a wise and godly man. He always imparted wisdom into his conversations and taught life lessons through his stories. On this particular day, Uncle Ed made a simple statement that has always stuck with me. He told me and my dad "Ask God into everything you do."

Simple yet profound.

I want you to notice the wording Uncle Ed used when he said "Ask God into *everything* You do."

He didn't say to ask God into church, but leave him out of work. Ask God into prayer, but don't say your prayers at school. Or ask God into your wedding, but leave him out of your marriage.

Nope, Uncle Ed said "Ask God into everything you do." He was not a man who minced words. He said what he meant and meant what he said. This means there are no exceptions as to which parts of your life God will play a role.

I believe Uncle Ed understood that we as human beings are also spiritual beings. We are created by God and created to be in relationship with God. There is nothing too big or too small in our lives to ask God into. That being said, here is something I believe Uncle Ed was passing on to us in that statement. Prayer is a vital component in life.

The Apostle Paul made a similar statement in his letter to the Church in Philippi "Don't worry about anything; instead, pray about everything. Tell God what you need, and thank him for all he has done." -Philippians 4:6

You see by asking God into everything, we are actually praying. That's what prayer is, a conversation with God. So, when we are asking God into everything, then we are by its very nature praying about everything. We are asking God to be in the midst of all we have going on and are doing in our lives.

If you ever had the blessing of listening to Uncle Ed pray, then you know he had an intimate relationship with God. You know he asked God into everything he did in his life. Uncle Ed talked the talk and walked the walk.

GAME CHANGING MOVE:

1. What areas of your life have you neglected to ask God into? Write them down in a journal.

2. Take the time right now to ask God into the areas you just wrote down.

3. Read *The Noticer* by Andy Andrews.

4. Write down Philippians 4:6 and Proverbs 3:6 on a notecard. Read these verses daily throughout the next week. Commit them to memory as you ask God into everything you do.

COACH P'S PRACTICE PLAN

Each day I type up a detailed practice plan for my wrestling team. Doing so allows me to get organized and stay on track in the midst of practice. The plan also serves as a guide for the team, helping them to clearly understand the expectations and mentally prepare for the workout they are about to undergo.

Admittedly, I don't always follow the practice plan to a tee. There are times when I read the team's body language and feel we must make adjustments in order to get the most out of that day's experience. Overall, the practice plan is developed to help each wrestler become the best version of themselves possible.

Coach Chad Parks and Shawnee Heights wrestler Carter Hall. (2014)

Here is one of my actual wrestling practice plans:

Wrestling Practice

Time	Activity
Pre	>Mental Training Notebooks
	>300 jump ropes
30m	Warm-up/Drills
5m	H2O
30m	Technique: Feet
	> Snap and cover to swing cradle
	Technique: Top
	> Cradle drill- Side by side, Inside, Cross face, Tripod
15m	> 5m drill match
	> 5m technique match (drill match with turns)
	> 5m play wrestle (situational creativity)
20m	Conditioning: Relay races and Sprints
10m	500 jump ropes
5m	Stretch
5m	Team Talk
Total Time	**2 hours**

Knowing this much detail and effort goes into preparing a wrestling practice, it only makes sense to do the same with life. Below I have prepared a practice plan for you, and it is to be completed daily. This practice plan can serve as a guide to help you stay organized, keep on track and mentally prepare each day.

There are times you will need to make adjustments to the plan in order to garner the greatest value from the experience. Implementing and completing this plan on a consistent basis will help you become the best version of you possible.

Your practice plan is as follows:

Life Practice

Time	Activity
Time	*Activity*
Pre	**Pray.** Take a few moments upon waking each morning and pray to God. Ask Him to bless you and thank Him for all He's done in your life.
Daily	**Believe the Promise.** God has great plans for your life, and He plans to use you mightily. You may not be able to see it right now, but that's okay. If God showed you His entire plan for your life, you'd be overwhelmed.
Daily	**Embrace the Process.** Life is more than outcomes; it's about the process. You must learn to embrace the process and understand that God has you on the Potter's wheel. You are the clay, and He is molding and remolding you into the vessel He desires you to become in order to fulfill His purposes.
Daily	**Use Your Platform.** God has given you a platform to use for His glory. You might be a parent, coach or NFL Football player. Each is a platform and each provides opportunity to influence others for good. Realize no matter where you are in life, there are people watching you and your moves will influence their lives.

"There are generations yet unborn, whose very lives will be shifted and shaped by the moves you make and the actions you take." -Andy Andrews

Daily   **Persevere with Passion.**
The most successful people in life are those who are determined to persevere with passion. This means you will keep on keepin on, no matter your current circumstances.
"I possess the greatest power ever bestowed upon mankind. I hold fast to my dreams. I stay the course. I do not quit." -Andy Andrews

Daily   **Peruse the Word.**
Read your Bible daily and watch God transform your heart, mind, and life. You will never have a deeper relationship with God or understanding of life than when you delve into the Word.

Scriptures for your practice plan:

Pray.

Jabez cried out to the God of Israel, "Oh, that you would bless me and enlarge my territory! Let your hand be with me, and keep me from harm so that I will be free from pain." And God granted his request. - 1 Chronicles 4:10

Believe the Promise.

For I know the plans I have for you," declares the LORD, "plans to prosper you and not to harm you, plans to give you hope and a future. -Jeremiah 29:11

Trust in the Lord with all you heart and lean not on your own understanding. In all your ways acknowledge Him and He'll direct your paths. -Proverbs 3:5-6

Embrace the Process.

This is the word that came to Jeremiah from the Lord: "Go down to the potter's house, and there I will give you my message." So I went down to the potter's house, and I saw him working at the wheel. But the pot he was shaping from the clay was marred in his hands; so the potter formed it into another pot, shaping it as seemed best to him. -Jeremiah 18: 1-4

Use Your Platform.

For we are God's handiwork, created in Christ Jesus to do good works, which God prepared in advance for us to do. -Ephesians 2:10

Persevere with Passion.

And let us not grow weary of doing good, for in due season we will reap, if we do not give up. -Galatians 6:9

Peruse the Word.

For the word of God is alive and active. Sharper than any double-edged sword, it penetrates even to dividing soul and spirit, joints and marrow; it judges the thoughts and attitudes of the heart. -Hebrews 4:12

GAME CHANGING MOVES:

1. Follow the practice plan above daily.

2. What is your platform? Write it down; determine to use it to glorify God and set a great example to everyone around you.

GAME CHANGING MOVES

My friend, it is no accident you read this book at this time in your life.

I believe God has prepared for you a series of game changing moves that will help both you and generations to come. It is my prayer that your heart was stirred by one or many of the life lessons I have learned on my journey and have shared in this book.

It is also my desire that you will pass on what you have learned to others. Knowledge and wisdom are not to be kept locked away in one's mind as only to benefit the keeper. No, knowledge and wisdom are to be passed on so they might profit the masses.

Thank you for investing your precious time into reading this. I suggest you read it again soon and watch as you learn something new the second time around. I hope the lessons I've shared will provide you with real and applicable principles you can apply to your life right away. May your journey be blessed and your game changing moves be abundant!

To get more game changing moves, visit and sign up for free content at coachchadparks.com

POSTSCRIPT

The moving force behind this book came from writing blogs over the last few years. Creating the content has allowed me to review my life and share with others the lessons I've learned along the way. The vast majority of these lessons have come through sports, hard work and relationships. What I didn't know when I originally started writing is that God would use the words to help encourage others.

Ultimately, I hope the lessons in this book have encouraged you. The word encourage actually means to inspire with courage, spirit or confidence. As a coach, I work hard to inspire my athletes with courage, lift their spirits, and provide confidence until they find their own. When all is said and done, the game changing move I hope this book has provided for you is to be encouraged!

"Therefore encourage one another and build each other up, just as in fact you are doing." - 1 Thessalonians 5:11

"A generous person will prosper; whoever refreshes others will be refreshed." -Proverbs 11:25

WHAT HAS WRESTLING GIVEN ME?

What has wrestling given me?
Stitches in both eyebrows and staples as well.
Nose broken multiple times with countless black eyes.
Stitches in my chin and chips in my front teeth, both top and bottom.
Cauliflower ears on both sides.
Broken fingers that no longer align.
Torn ligaments in my wrist, knees and ankle.
Knee drained every week for months.
Two knee surgeries, two big toe surgeries and a nose surgery.
Broken ribs with torn cartilage in between.
These are a few of my favorite things (not really).
Wrestling has given me physical injuries from my head to my toes.
It has dealt out pain from a countless number of blows.

Yet with everything my body has endured, wrestling
has given so much more.

Chad Parks the day after a college wrestling tournament. (2000)

What has wrestling given me?
Strength in my body and also in mind.
Courage to take on every challenge.
Skills to defend myself and protect others.
Love in action from my father and mother.
Knowledge that I'm not always in control.
Evidence that I will reap what I sow.
Discipline to do what the average person won't.
Love for the process of trying to become great.
Respect for others who've been in my place.
Teammates turned family, for they are more than friends.
They are my brothers through thick and thin.
Opportunities to travel all around the nation.
Connections with others who share this infatuation.
Confidence that comes from conquering fears.
Passion galore, in the form of laughter or tears.
Unmatched work ethic to back up my dreams.
These are a few of my favorite things.

The Parks Family (Chad, Laurie, Kate, Ally, Luke, and Jake). (2015)

What has wrestling given me?
All that I've listed and so much more.
Everything on this list is real and true, but one question remains...
What has wrestling given you?

God Bless,
Coach P

"So Jacob was left alone, and a man wrestled with him till daybreak. When the man saw that he could not overpower him, he touched the socket of Jacob's hip so that his hip was wrenched as he wrestled with the man." Genesis 32:24-25

GAME CHANGERS CREED

I am a Game Changer and called to live for a higher purpose.
Today I am dedicated to becoming the best version of myself in
order to glorify God.
I will pray, pursue wisdom and persevere with passion.
I will build into the lives of others and love them with all my heart.
I will walk in gratitude and enjoy each moment because it is a
gift from above.
No perceived limitation will limit me as my God will make a way.
I will control what I can control and refuse to worry about the rest.
I am dedicated to the vision and mission God has placed upon
my heart.
I will dream so big that the dream cannot be accomplished without
God's help.
I am a person of action and strive to be the hardest worker in the
room at all times.
Iron sharpens iron, so I will surround myself with high level
human beings.
I will be a light both in my home and in my community.
I will fight the good fight for what matters most.
I am a Game Changer and today I will enact Game Changing Moves!

SUGGESTED READING

1. *The Bible*, by God
2. *An Impractical Guide to Becoming a Transformational Leader*, by Jamie Gilbert and Joshua Medcalf
3. *The Noticer*, by Andy Andrews
4. *Greater*, by Steven Furtick
5. *The Mentor Leader*, by Tony Dungy
6. *Chase the Lion*, by Mark Batterson
7. *2 Chairs*, by Bob Beaudine
8. *The Greatest Salesman in the World*, by Og Mandino
9. *The Happiness Advantage*, by Shawn Achor
10. *The Carpenter*, by Jon Gordon
11. *Chop Wood Carry Water*, by Joshua Medcalf
12. *(Un)Qualified*, by Steven Furtick
13. *Start*, by Jon Acuff
14. *The Wrestler*, by Michael Fessler
15. *Mind of the Athlete*, by Dr. Jarrod Spencer

ACKNOWLEDGEMENTS

To God- thank you for sending your son Jesus to die on the cross in my place so that I might be saved. Your love, grace, and strength amaze me each and every day.

To my wife, Laurie- thank you for being my rock and supporting me as I pursue the dreams God has placed in my heart. You are a true champion and my best friend.

To Kate, Ally, Luke, and Jake- thank you for making me a better coach and father. I love you more than words can express.

To my mom and dad, Martin and LaCrecia Parks- thank you for loving and guiding me throughout my life. God has blessed me with a tremendous family.

To Bob and Sharon Meissner- thank you for loving and being there for my family.

To Tony Killscrow- thank you for showing me how to live for Jesus with passion and action.

To Carl and LaVerne Core- thank you for loving me and showing me by example how to connect to the heart through building relationships.

To Paula Mashunkashey- thank you for building me up with kind words, prayer, and love throughout much of my life. Your enthusiasm for Jesus shines so brightly that those around you need to wear shades.

To all of my coaches, mentors and leaders- thank you for investing in my life and sharing your precious wisdom with me. It's not even fair how many awesome people God has placed in my path to help me learn about true relational leadership.

To every athlete, I've had the opportunity to coach and the men I've coached with- thank you for your dedication and love. It's truly an honor to work with each and every one of you.

To Tanner Gardner- thank you for writing such an awesome foreword for this book. You inspire everyone around you and bring them to a new level. It's a blessing to call you a friend.

To Bill Kentling and Cody Foster- thank you for your help with this book and for believing in me. When this idea only existed in the realm of possibility, you helped bring it into the land of reality.

To Gordon Thiessen and Cross Training Publishing- thank you for believing in me, this book, and for your ministry. Words cannot adequately express the gratitude I have in my heart for you.

To Joe Hansen- thank you for the awesome cover design and the willingness to put my ideas into art.

To you- thank you for taking the time to read this book; I am honored. I hope it proves to be a valuable resource you can use in your life and share with others.

ABOUT THE AUTHOR

Chad Parks is a wrestling coach, teacher and strength training specialist. Also a renowned speaker, he has dedicated his life to inspiring others to reach their fullest potential through life in Jesus.

Chad and his wife Laurie reside in Topeka, KS with their four children. As a couple, they are involved in various ministries throughout the greater Topeka area, such as Fellowship of Christian Athletes, Young Life and Wrestlers for Christ.

Connect with Chad

Feel free to connect with Chad on his website, through email, or via social media at the addresses below:

Website: http://coachchadparks.com/
E-mail: coachchadparks@gmail.com
Facebook: https://www.facebook.com/coachchadparks/
Twitter: @coachchadparks
Instagram: coachchadparks